25 ways to become your own psychiatrist

A Little life guide to sidestep years of therapy and medication

DR. DIEGO CARRANZA TRESOLDI

To Heather, always...

*To my patients, on behalf of whom
I wrote this book.*

To my parents, Norah and Ñato.

*To Miss Monica, Miss Pamela,
And all my dear British School
teachers*

Introduction

I will begin by clarifying that I have nothing against mental health professionals, especially since I am one of them.

This book, the title of which could be interpreted as provocative, is not meant in any way as an anti-psychiatry, anti-psychotherapy or anti-psychopharmaceutical manifesto.
This book is not only connected with my experiences as a psychiatrist, it also includes concepts and ideas based on my personal experiences, the result of a professional journey through 4 different countries in which I trained and gained valuable experience after graduating in medicine: My native Argentina and the USA where I trained as a general / digestive surgeon; France where I followed my training as a cardiovascular / thoracic surgeon and finally Spain, my adoptive homeland where both circumstance coupled with a persistent passion and interest in self-care and therapy triggered me to explore a new field of medicine and retrain as a psychiatrist.
This is not necessarily a self-help book, Or maybe it is. The importance lies in whether it is helpful to anyone.

A traditional self-help book by definition implies that we sometimes need help to be happy. A list that proposes a variety of ways to improve our lives suggests, precisely, that our life may require "improvements." The desire to "fix" presupposes that we may be 'broken'. However, people should not be compared to machines that can be broken or repaired by simply reading some instructions!

This book, however, even though it also lists a series of items, presents the argument that we can be happy (or at least psychologically healthy) on our own, using our own emotional tools. It is also plausible that maybe we are already happy and we have not realized it!

This is a book that aims to contrast common sense with the irrational, and draw attention to life habits that can at times weigh down our well-being, daily routines and behaviours that we have learnt without even questioning them.

Every day patients come to my practice some with conditions that require psychotropic drugs to be administered in order to improve their quality of life and even save lives: schizophrenia, bipolar disorder, phobias, endogenous depression... **evidence-based medicine continues to prove convincingly and beyond any doubt that drugs and psychotherapy work in these cases and continue to change lives for the better.** With reference to these cases, I do everything possible to encourage patients and relatives to accept help including any other psychic pathology that proves a source of disability.

But the complexity and social pressures of current life continue to bring to consultation a variety of patients; people seeking guidance who are trying to find a solution to their daily-

life problems through medication, people who doubt their own abilities in the face of unforeseen challenges that life throws at us...

These are people who are sometimes looking for a sort of "magic pill" to solve their problems, but at the same time they do not want to feel "detached and without feeling". There are also people who ask for "guidelines or ideas" to face the difficulties that life puts in their path. They often seek someone to act as an "emotional coach" who, they hope, will somehow illuminate their path and offer more clarity to complex and challenging situations.

The present work is dedicated to them. Not to become their designated coach, but with the aim to provide advice, reflection and strategies to help them overcome difficult situations.

I believe that many emotional problems derive from learned behaviors or concepts, essentially from parents, teachers, peers and the media, and that people can unlearn these patterns for themselves. In many cases even, professional help can become redundant or even counterproductive, "psychologizing" (over analyzing and obstructing) daily life situations. If people realize that they play a crucial role in overcoming their problems, "common sense-based self-therapy" can become a highly effective option.

The psychiatry in which I adhere to, and which I try to practice and teach, places the patient as co-responsible for their treatment, informing them in the most respectful way about their symptoms and the existing solutions, encouraging them to choose between the different therapeutic tools available, and empowering them to become their own 'actor' of their improvement. Sometimes it is easy to overlook the most important authority: yourself. If your own inner guidance as a source of wisdom is overlooked, your course of action may prove ineffective and even lead to unnecessary complications. Positive psychology and psychiatry, (becoming your own expert in the illness itself) along with behavioral and cognitive therapies, recognized today as effective in many pathologies are based on this philosophy of collaborative care; an informed and active patient who is making their own decisions. A patient who shows improvement is a patient who has reached a level of understanding of how they function psychologically and emotionally. They have learnt strategies to help prevent, manage and cope with their vulnerabilities and adversities, present or future. This is a patient who is his own best psychiatrist!

It is true that the added support of a psychotherapist provides an objective and external vision, providing technical and human skills in complicated situations. However, all effective therapies aim primarily at the development of three essential things: self-knowledge, self-sufficiency and self-management processes. In fact, the human mind is endowed with many capacities and resilience that allow, without realizing at times, a solution to many problems and these skills, possibly assisted by an external guide, can also help to correct bad habits acquired over time.

It is with all this in mind that I wrote this book. It is driven by modern scientific knowledge alongside my personal life experience and professional experience as a physician and therapist. I have aimed to incorporate principles and effective strategies that can be applied by oneself, independently or with the professional treatment of a mental health practitioner at the same time. Of course, independent intervention requires having understood and accepted certain psychological mechanisms, which does not happen overnight.

It is for this reason that each chapter contains quite detailed explanations of the concepts that are discussed before addressing the means to deal with them. All are accompanied by practical examples inspired by real cases of my daily practice, although with fictitious names and situations.

You will also note that I often place emphasis on the fact that progress occurs in stages over time and alongside effort and determination a certain amount of "discipline", is also required but the results will definitely be worth it.

In short: This book is about how to approach common place ideas and habits, which are not necessarily productive or conducive to happiness but rather the opposite. These conceptions can be modified by adopting a more positive approach.

Certain phobias, anxieties, manias or blockades, tend to be socially accepted and / or tolerated, which can lead them to become embedded in our psyche, thus hindering the change process. This can become demoralizing for us and eventually wear us down; A bit like a stone in the shoe that we decide not to remove. It allows us to walk, but slowly and with unnecessary pain.

Dr. Diego Carranza Tresoldi

Dr. Diego Carranza Tresoldi has a degree in medicine and surgery, he specialized in digestive surgery at the National University of Córdoba (Argentina), has a fellowship in surgery and endoscopy at Norwalk Hospital, (USA) and was Chef de clinique in cardiovascular and thoracic surgery at the Louis Pasteur University of Strasbourg (France).

• He Specialized in psychiatry at the Vega Baja Hospital, Orihuela-Spain.

• He is also the author of "Survival Guide for Psychiatry Residents" Amazon, 2019) and "Simplified Psychiatry" (Amazon, 2019)

• He Currently practices psychiatry privately in Alicante, Murcia and Torrevieja (Spain)

• Comments and suggestions: diegocarranza@yahoo.com

Table of contents

1. Dare to be disliked

You would not worry so much about what others think of you if you realized how little they do
-Eleanor Roosevelt

Ana is a 42-year-old mother of 2 children, 11 and 13. She works full-time as a nurse. She is 30 kilograms over her desired weight and struggles to follow the diet prescribed by her nutritionist, so we sit down to discuss a way forward. She reveals that she has not started exercising or keeping a diet diary (as recommended by her nutritionist) and that that she continues to eat fast food on a regular basis. "I'm very busy," she said. "My only opportunity to exercise is to wake up at 5.00 am and go for a walk; but once I am up, I realize how much I have to do. I spend my time preparing meals, on the computer answering emails from my father's business and cleaning the house. I am unable to exercise after work because I have to take my children directly to football practice. When we arrive home, they are hungry, so I just prepare something quickly if I have not planned dinner in advance. This makes me feel guilty and I then start planning the meal for the next day. Before I know it, it is 9 o'clock at night and I am ready to go to sleep. In addition, I have to go to the nursing home to see my mother-in-law twice a week, which I tend to do at the weekend or on a day when the children do not have a football game. Also, last month a friend asked me to help her paint her house and my sister wants me to help with a house move. "I'm exhausted! I just do not have time for anything else."

And indeed, Ana did not have time for herself as her own needs were overlooked because she wanted to please everyone else. It took several months of intense work to bring to light a pattern of "indulging at all costs" by helping Ana to find the way to healthy selfishness, but we succeeded.

Ana currently weighs 15 kilos less. Her sister, her friend and her mother-in-law stopped talking to her for a while, but in time they adapted to the situation. Ana was relieved when she regained her relationship with the three of them (although this time under her own conditions), and she came to the conclusion that "she was not too worried about the matter either." What mattered most to her now was herself and her well-being. And interestingly, she expressed that people appeared to appreciate her more like that.

Many "compliant" people can disguise their attitude with kindness. When they talk about their reluctance to say no, it is common for them to say things like "I do not want to look selfish" or "I'm so silly."

At times, people not only take advantage of us in an unkind way, sometimes they do it just because they feel they have the authority to do so or because we make it too easy for them by allowing them to.

Constantly trying to please people can be a serious problem, and an increasingly hard habit to break.

Even though people could view this as selfish, how could I help others if I did not take care of my own physical and psychological health first? Taking care and control of our own well-being places us in a stronger position to do things that benefit others.

In consultation, I often refer to the analogy of the airplane: Before taking off, the air crew tell us that, if the oxygen masks fall in case of emergency, we must immediately use them first ourselves to then be able to help the person sat next to us.

Fear appears to be the biggest obstacle when it comes to changing our attitude into the kind of healthy selfishness that benefits us and everyone we know. Fear of hurting others, fear of being judged, fear of being rejected, fear of losing the love of someone we care about, fear of being left alone...

Healthy egoism can be perceived as risk taking, as it tends to worry us how we will be perceived by others. However, this does not mean that we are ignoring the feelings and needs of other people. It means that we care about ourselves and value our needs, desires, feelings and dreams before those of others.

The more recent unpredictable work market, is an area in which we are encouraged to "not be selfish". Recruiters tend to advertise towards those "with a desire to work, placing emphasis on enthusiasm and team spirit"; Sometimes the reality is the opposite and people can end up postponing their own dreams in pursuit of the employer's demands, meaning the employer (i.e. management) are able to lead without moral principles or scruples.

Is it wrong to set limits to a boss's irrational or unprofessional demands? Maybe not. Of course, there is always the fear of being dismissed from your job, although in some cases, the result of this may actually be in your favor: Instead of suffering unjustifiable stress and duress over long periods we could attempt to find another type of employment which leads us to feel even more satisfied with ourselves. It is also worth considering, that those people in similar situations who stay in fear of losing their job may also wish they had the strength and opportunity to be more proactive. Are we selfish when we say no to a neighbour who is intrusive, demands "favors" and refuses to acknowledge that they are bothering others by continually playing loud music throughout the day? This is definitely not the case. The 'unhealthy' egoist is the one, who only thinks about their own wellbeing with little or no regard for others.

Are we undermining our relationship when we express frustration towards our partner who is not willing to contribute to the running of the home? Definitely not, we should be working together towards a more balanced and mutually respectful relationship.

How many teenagers suffer today because they have not been taught that it is not necessary to be "part of the cool crowd" and that it is enough to be themselves, without changing their way of being or thinking to belong to a group or not to be judged?

The following are 10 signs to illustrate how we may be trying too hard to please:

1. We pretend to agree with everyone.

Listening politely to other people's opinions, even if you do not agree, demonstrates social skill. On the other hand, pretending or alluding to agree only to please others can lead us to betray our principles.

2. We feel responsible for how other people feel.

It is healthy to recognize how our behavior can have a direct influence on others. However, to think that we have the power to make someone happy or miserable is a problem. Each person is responsible for their own emotions.

3. We often apologize.

Whether we blame ourselves frequently, or whether blame is attributed by others, repeated apologies can be a sign of a bigger problem. We do not have to regret being ourselves (However, we are in control of our actions and sometimes we need to apologize for these).

4. We feel overwhelmed by the things we have to do.

We are each responsible for how we spend our time. If we constantly seek to please people, it is very likely that our agenda is full of activities that we believe other people want us to do.

5. We are unable to say no to anyone.
It is ok to avoid ruffling feathers, but at what cost? Personal integrity and self-respect? Peace of mind? Sometimes "no" is the most honorable and respectful thing you can say to someone.

6. We feel uncomfortable if someone is angry or disappointed with us.
Just because someone is angry with you does not necessarily mean you did something wrong. Nonetheless, if we cannot bear the idea that someone is angry with us, we will be more likely to give in frequently.

7. We act like the people around us.
Mimetizing ourselves with others to be accepted may not be a good idea for our self-esteem. Let's start by accepting and celebrating that we are different, unique and unrepeatable.

8. We need validation to feel good.
While words of praise and kindness are needed to make us feel good and valued, some people rely too heavily on validation. If our self-esteem rests entirely on what others think, our emotional balance can be weakened.

9. We do everything possible to avoid conflicts.
It is one thing to not enjoy being confrontational with someone. On the other hand, avoiding conflicts at all costs could potentially lead us to stop fighting for the values we have and the people we believe in.

10. We do not admit when our feelings are hurt.

To maintain deep relationships with others we must create an environment that enables us to talk about our feelings. Denying that we are angry, sad, ashamed or disappointed, even if we feel emotionally hurt, makes our relationships superficial.

How to proceed if we can identify with any of the above discussion points?

Try to accept that you can't please everyone. Saying "yes" to everything and everyone can not only leave you in a vulnerable position, it can also give rise to more complicated situations and bad feeling. Being true to ourselves and others means validating what we feel, expressing our honesty and accepting that not everyone will agree with us or see the world in the same way that we do. Disagreement in a cordial and somewhat assertive way can make life much simpler.

In discovering that any relationship problems reflect an internal conflict we also find that the relationship process itself is a means to know and understand ourselves more clearly. Any problems that we can identify in relation to our more unconscious resistance pave the way to acceptance of our more inaccessible conflicts.

Recognize that the strive for external recognition can be an ego trap.

Instead of seeking recognition and consolation from others, it may be more convenient to recognize ourselves as we are, to find out why we refuse to validate and celebrate what we already are instead of yearning for what we may never be.

Helping someone because it gives us pleasure is one thing. Solely doing it with the aim and hope that people have a better impression of us is something very different.

Live life in our own way

We are taught and encouraged to live according to the points of view, desires, direction and perception of others. Taking a step back to observe and meditate on what we really desire out of life is a journey that invites reflection and one that can beneficially transform our lives.

Don't be afraid to question everything in search of the truth

There is no valid excuse to hide from the truth. We can only begin to see through the fog when the ego becomes both a friend and a teacher.

2. Deal with toxic people in your life

Let go of the people who only come to share complaints, problems, disaster stories, fear and judgment of others. If somebody is looking for a boat where to throw their trash, try for it not to be your mind.
-Dalai Lama

This section is intended to provide an overview of attitudes that characterize people with certain personality traits, those of which can make things more difficult in everyday life.

Interpersonal relationships are complex and in general when we talk about toxic people, we refer to people who exhibit dysfunctional traits in their behavior. While this is not defined specifically as a personality disorder, it is better understood as a rigid and dysfunctional pattern of behavior that affects the life of the person in terms of their environment and all areas of their life: Family and personal relationships both at home and at work.

It's understandable that many relationships, particularly family ones are difficult to manage because it is not easy to confront or shut out a member of the family who displays these types of characteristics. However, if we continually feel bad about ourselves as a result of a relationship with this person then it is time to sit down and evaluate the problem.

It is important to note that at times, their dysfunctional behavior patterns can cloud our judgement. However, rather than continue to suffer in silence, it is more important to address and deal with the problem: **It is more important to protect yourself rather than dwell on the reasons for their behavior.**

These people may not change their behavior, in spite of suffering from a disorder and especially without any professional help. They may have a distorted view with regard to what a healthy relationship consists of. Others have even learnt their behavior which results in taking advantage of others and they even enjoy it. Unfortunately, the ones who can end up suffering the most are the people around them, but we can adopt another approach.

Whatever the reasons, the following is vital: **It is better to protect and believe in ourselves in the face of self-doubt.**

Maybe we all have the ability to become toxic in certain relationships. Here, the emphasis would be on 'toxic relationships' in which the emotional distress prevails due to the attitudes assumed. However, those people who manifest toxic behaviors more often do so because they have developed relational habits that are often with intent, harmful to others.

We will all know of or have met a toxic person at some point in our lives and dealing with this can be emotionally draining to say the least. In fact, it can challenge what we know (or what we think we know about ourselves) as well as test and push our limits of tolerance.

Here are some general features to observe and to note that most of these traits are compatible with Narcissistic Personality Disorder.

Toxic people are manipulative. Their primary objective is to make people do what they want them to do with the focus primarily on themselves – it is all about them. They use other people to achieve whatever their goal is. When we bond or have a relationship with them it is not about a fair or equal relationship, in fact it's much less.

They are critical. We need to be alert in terms of what they think we have or haven't done. The problem rarely lies with themselves and they will lie or invent things if it helps them to gain or win from the situation. **They do not take responsibility for their own feelings.** Quite the opposite as they tend to project their feelings and emotions onto others. If you try to point this out to them, they are likely to vehemently defend their position without taking any responsibility for their actions. They will even go as far as to accuse others for their own faults and label them as 'selfish' or 'irrational'. This projection of behavior usually serves to provoke anger, which is a position in which they feel very comfortable. Their provocation of anger and helplessness also provides them with their perfect stimulus and response, "See how **you** behave/get?"

They rarely apologize. They do not see any reason to apologize because they place the blame elsewhere. In many cases, they tend to manipulate their environment for their own purposes and try to gain sympathy and attention by claiming 'victim' status. The fault will always lie with others because the alternative, which involves recognizing their own responsibility is inadmissible.

They are inconsistent. It can be hard to understand who we are at any given time because they are often not the same person. Their perspective, behavior and attitude can change depending on what they want to achieve. They also know how to be nice and how to charm when they want something from others.

They are constantly testing us. Toxic characters also make others choose between them or someone else, or between something they want and something we want. This can often become a 'divide and conquer tactic' where the only valid option is themselves even to the point or at the cost of requiring others to break a relationship in order to satisfy themselves.

They put us on the defensive. They find difficulty in focusing on certain issues that are not in their interest. They are often not interested in our point of view or in reaching an amicable conclusion. Remember: They have the ability to be extreme manipulators and their tactics can include vagueness and irrationality, singing their own praises, projecting and shifting the spotlight onto others, justifying and focusing on problems rather than solutions, etc.

They often do not care, do not support or are not interested in the things that are important to others. In fact, good things that happen to others divert attention from themselves and prevent them from focusing on their own goals. Loyalty is a concept that they demand but often struggle with themselves.

They can often pretend that others solve their problems. They would like us to feel sorry for them and be responsible for what happens to them. However, after each crisis your problems are never really solved as inevitably there is another to follow. What they really crave is our constant support and sympathy and they will create one drama after another to achieve it. "Helping them or rescuing them" fails to work especially when those involved are more interested in finding solutions than the toxic person themselves.

Toxic behavior can both drain and feed on people's emotions and spending time with these people can leave us feeling emotionally drained. It is constantly about taking care of the problems they create which can leave people feeling frustrated, unsatisfied or even angry. It is important not to let yourself reach that level of exhaustion. Initially, you may feel compassion but after a time of negative interactions it is better to take an emotional and/or physical distance. Remember that our time and energy are essential components to our own well-being and they should not be spent on wasted or futile situations.

Therefore, it is useful to know how to prepare and protect yourself with some basic skills.

Controlled exposure to situations.

The safest way to protect yourself from toxic behavior is undoubtedly by limiting or suspending the time spent with the person(s) involved although at times this is not possible or practical. For example, if we work in a toxic environment, we can request a new project or area of work. If this is not possible, alert your boss to the situation and request any necessary modifications. If the toxic person happens to be your boss try to minimize contact as much as possible. Again, if this is not an option report the circumstances to the appropriate person so the situation can be monitored and recorded. If this still proves too difficult it may be work considering or looking for alternative employment.

For those responsible for recruiting new staff it is important to pay special attention during the interview process to the emotional stability and competence of candidates as well as establish clear rules of behavior and expectations from the offset.

Managing awareness and reactions

This is where attitudes and behavior toward toxic situations and people can help protect you from the negative connotations and affects that prevail. It essentially consists of setting clear limitations in order to avoid being locked in on-going emotional battles and games. Say "No" firmly to any requests that you consider unreasonable, without providing a justification. For example, "I am not going to have this conversation if you continue to use an ironic and/or insulting tone" or " I think we'll leave this conversation for another time when you are calmer".

In relation to situations in the work place, it is advisable to keep a personal diary/record of each discussion, with the date and time, so that any inappropriate behavior over any duration of time can be referred to and acted on by the relevant investigating personnel.

Strengthen ties with relatives and close friends, especially if the toxic situation(s) is caused by a partner. Having our point of view validated can also help improve our self-esteem and counteract feelings of isolation.

It is vital to look for activities that take us away from the toxic person/situation so that we do not lose the idea of who we are and what we stand for in relation to the world we live in.

Do not give explanations

By definition, a toxic person is the one who refuses to listen to our perspective. Attempts to explain or justify ourselves will only lead to frustration. We can say, "I'm sorry, but I am busy " or "At the moment I am unable to speak to you" or quite simply and in a calm manner

"I do not have to give you any explanation in relation to this conversation".

Protect/Immunize ourselves

It is advisable to be alert in order to detect and recognize those with toxic potential in order to avoid incidences occurring. Recognize the personality traits that feed toxic situations: "Queens/Kings of drama", "Manipulation Masters" who are full of resentment and who tend not to be interested in the feelings and needs of others...

Amalia's life hadn't been easy since she met Héctor. They had been together for 15 years and they had one son. She was 54 years old and he was 69.

Héctor had been a successful business man, he had few or no friends, his former employees showed little appreciation for him; he had a domineering and authoritative character and was quite arrogant, although according to Amalia, "deep down he was a beautiful person".

Amalia fell into a deep depression, to which she had no explanation.

The hidden secrets of their circumstances were soon to be revealed. Héctor, who had always been occupied with work and away from home had recently retired. Now Amalia was the working parent, not because she needed to, as she had put her career on hold to bring up her children but because she wanted to work. Now was the time for her to fill fulfilled and she had started to work on her own collection of designs for the decoration industry.

Héctor was not happy with this change of circumstances; besides that, he struggled with the fact that he no longer had anyone to give orders to; now he had to accept that he was no longer solely responsible for supporting the family financially.

Hector's known passive-aggressive attitude now changed into harassment and insults. Every time that Amalia went on work-related trips the discussions became for intense. Héctor reclaimed his "right to be happy" and he emotionally manipulated Amalia, using their son as ammunition by stating that his school work was suffering since she had returned to work (this was not the case in fact quite the opposite). Then came the suicide threats from Héctor which caused Amalia intense anxiety to the point of which she started to take medication in order to sleep. She felt an immense guilt and accepted every word from Héctor as the truth. When Amalia seeked professional help, Héctor also went to see a psychiatrist because in his own words "I can no longer suffer my wife's authoritative manner".

Very gradually, Amalia began to become more aware of the emotional trap that she had fallen into: Her husband revealed toxic traits and if she hadn't realized this before it was because they hadn't spent a lot of quality time together. His motives became uncovered as soon as Amalia had wanted to return to work and have her own independence.

His despotic and childish attitude was gaining in intensity until one day Hector decided to show up at an exhibition mounted by Amalia; he took the microphone and began to speak to the audience crying while telling how his wife had ruined his life, "neglecting his own family "

After witnessing this, she decided to file for divorce. Since the day He left the house she has not taken antidepressants again.

Hector also abandoned the treatment but not before threatening with legal action towards his psychiatrist if he did not testify against his wife.

3. Differentiate between real and fabricated threats

Of all the liars in the world, sometimes the worst are our own fears.
-Rudyard Kipling

There is no hell more intolerable than the one we create ourselves. We live anticipating the worst. Our brain, according to neuroscientists, is designed to survive the dangers that lurked at the dawn of human existence. In prehistoric times, if the leaves of a bush seemed to move, it was better to flee just in case it was a predator than to remain still, thinking that it was because of the wind.

Today there are no more saber-toothed tigers lurking around the corner. The primitive reflection that protected us has ceased to be necessary and can sometimes even be harmful.

Will I lose my job? Will my partner leave me? What if something happens to my children? All these uncertainties generated tend to perpetuate, forming an anxiety loop that is challenging to break. When the feeling of fear invades us, our body triggers a series of reactions to protect us and prepare for flight. The heart pumps harder and faster if there is a need to run; sweat is produced, breathing is accelerated, the digestive system and the immune system stop spending energy. Everything is set up in case it is necessary to fight or flee. A large amount of blood is derived from organs to other parts of the body so we can run away if needed.

Anticipation leads to anxiety, and anxiety leads to depression.

Imaginary dangers generate organic and psychological wear due to specific automatic associations that we reinforce by performing them frequently without being aware of it.

It is essential to accept that the more we anticipate that things might happen, they will. Getting ahead of events, therefore, may well be an adaptive trait, but sometimes it can turn against us.

Mindfulness, a technique of recognized efficacy today, is neither new nor a recent invention. It was practiced in ancient times by Buddhist monks, Hindus, and even the Celts. Over the years, it has been given various names: Mind control, meditation, transcendental meditation

Its foundation serves to place full attention to the present moment, leaving aside the past that weighs on us and the future that worries us so much. Studies have revealed excellent results when consistently applied.

Andrew was a 29-year-old bank employee who came to my office complaining about insomnia and anxiety. He had been on occupational leave for three months and sometimes could not get up before noon. Antidepressants and anxiolytics were not working.

Throughout therapy, it became clear that Andrew presented a vital pattern of anticipation, perhaps validated by his family environment, which he described as "anxious."

He told me that before falling asleep, he imagined the worst possible situations that could happen at work, which was the only financial means of family support. A few months ago, the company he worked at had hired a "human resources specialist" who would be responsible for "rationalizing the workforce," which, according to Andrés, was a euphemism for "Everybody is getting the boot." Since then, he felt that his boss had changed his attitude and was avoiding him. He believed that his coworkers also treated him differently, and he was sure that he would be fired.

He began to imagine what his life would be like for his wife if he became ill or without their children, "with so many dangers in this unpredictable world..." Andrew admitted that he generally tended to anticipate the worst. Over time, we worked on the idea of spotting out negativity; he began to realize that generally, the chances of something horrible happening rarely come true. Andrés had not been aware of this and was continuously renewing hypothetical and catastrophic scenarios without even realizing it.

In another ordering of events regarding his situation in the company, we concluded that in the worst case, other job options had not been taken into account. We also worked on the possibility that his own mind was

"playing tricks" on him. Maybe they were not really going to fire him, and the company was just trying to improve productivity, which ended up being the case. Being aware of the situation was the first step of a long road ahead. My first recommendation was to attend mindfulness sessions. Over time, he came to confess a healthy addiction.
Little by little, we started reducing medication.

Certain anticipatory neurotic ideas tend to persist in our ever-busy mind. We can keep them under control by repeating each time we imagine a catastrophe: "Only when I get to that bridge will I cross it."
Identifying these "irrational" thoughts is critical. **It is essential to realize that the vast majority of what we imagine never happens.** And even if it happens, we probably couldn't do anything to avoid it. The healthy attitude would be, therefore, **"to take care of business rather than worry."**
Just as the mind can activate these anxiety pathways, we must use our imagination to redirect or "reset" them.

If we can imagine everything negative that could happen to us, we can also choose to think that the opposite can also occur.

4. Rather than complain be grateful for what you have

Be thankful for what you have; you'll end up having more. If you concentrate on what you don't have, you will never, ever have enough.
-Oprah Winfrey

A Persian proverb reads, "I cursed the fact of not having shoes until I met a man who had no feet."
Simple things like being healthy, walking, having food every day, loving and being loved, having a job should not, in any case, be taken for granted.
Some may say that this implies conformity, but it is undeniable that this is an essential adaptive feature.
If our mind can choose what to focus on, why focus on what we don't have, what we lack, the negative side of things?
In doing so, we would focus on limitations, on desires, on expectations that are never fulfilled, committing the fateful mistake of ignoring the unquestionable abundance in which we live.
And it's not just about avoiding the act of complaining: **Nothing attracts our attention more than what we are trying to elude.** It is more productive to

exercise, to identify the moments in which we focus on the negative, and systematically oppose something for which we are grateful. The repetitive exercise of this technique works wonders.

The testimonies of survivors of Nazi concentration camps are eloquent: they speak of those who could abstract themselves from horror by focusing their attention on a flower growing alongside the road to the labor camp, a sunbeam entering through the broken window of the barracks, a friendly hand approaching a piece of bread... Similar to everyday life, survival in extreme situations like this is based on simple things: being thankful for what we do have.

The benefits of gratitude have always been known. It is not about simplistic and puerile positive psychology; these benefits have even been scientifically researched. One of these studies is by Robert Emmons and Michael McCullough, reflected in his book "*The Psychology of Gratitude* "[1].

Four subgroups were formed randomly.

• Before bedtime, the members of the first group were asked to write down five things that occurred throughout the day for which they felt grateful.

• The second group was asked to record five negative things that had happened to them.

• The third group would list five things they considered to have done better than others that day.

• Finally, the members of the fourth group (or control group) should point out five things, negative or positive, that had happened to them during the day.

The degree of life satisfaction expressed by the participants during the study was then measured by Including how happy they said they were, their level of optimism, the effectiveness in achieving their goals, their state of physical health and how generous/benevolent they were. The group that revealed the worst results in all the measurements was the one that pointed out five problems every night. In contrast, the most positive results in satisfaction, optimism, success in achieving their goals, healthy physical condition, and a high degree of benevolence and generosity were exhibited by those who wrote down five reasons every night for which they felt grateful.

Antonio is a 45-year-old financial adviser; he started therapy because of his depression and alcohol addiction.
His marital life was in trouble, and he could not find the motivation to work. He was irritable, and he was not having any quality time with his son. His self-esteem was really low because he could not stop drinking. He was using alcohol to hide what he considered was wrong in his life and overwhelmed him.
The therapy was barely progressing; despite Antonio's courage and commitment, the results were modest.
One day, he decided to take a weekend off in the countryside to meditate over his problems; he went

for a walk in the mountains early in the morning. It was dark, and he slipped; he fell down a 20-meter high ravine.

He spent a few days at the hospital with some fractures, and he lost his cell phone. But the most important consequence of the near-death experience was that he became mindful of everything that was positive in his life: he had formed a family, had a job, had friends, and was alive, and he was grateful for these.

The incident was not miraculous, but it was the trigger for progressive and sustained improvement.

When I reflect on this, I like to remember a Chinese proverb that states happiness is not about desiring what we would like, but about loving what we do have. In other words, happiness is an attitude towards life; it's the way we deal with it. So is success.

Focusing on what we have instead of stopping at what we want is one of the ways to deal with life and one of the paths to happiness and personal satisfaction. **Gratitude, therefore, far from being a dispensable emotion, is an attitude we adopt toward life, and it contributes to improving self-esteem.** It also improves our ties with others, helps us to cope with stress and adversity, inhibits unfavorable comparisons with the environment, and stimulates us to adapt to new circumstances.

5. Do not wait to feel good to be ok

The best way to not feel hopeless is to get up and do something. Don't wait for good things to happen to you. If you go out and make some good things happen, you will fill the world with hope, you will fill yourself with hope.
 -**Barack Obama**

Every time people smile, their brains throw a little party. For starters, their smiles trigger the release of neuropeptides that work to combat stress. Neuropeptides are tiny molecules that allow neurons to communicate. They make it easier to send messages to the whole body when one is happy, sad, angry, depressed or excited. "Wellness" neurotransmitters, dopamine, endorphins and serotonin, are released when one smiles. This not only relaxes the body but can also lower the heart rate and blood pressure.
Endorphins also act as natural painkillers and antidepressants.
A smile causes serotonin release, which mimics the action of an antidepressant. Indeed, many of the antidepressants available today act on these "neurological messengers." But they do so at a cost: there are certain occasional side effects.

The brain itself does not differentiate between a false smile and a spontaneous one, which makes people think that it is possible to "deceive" it.

By analogy, the same is true about physical activity. People tend to think that, because they are slightly depressed or anxious (obviously, we are not talking about severe cases with functional repercussions here), it is not possible to stay active or take part in pleasant activities. In fact, the nervous system works the other way around: the more messages the body sends that one is moving about, the faster that mood recovery occurs.

It's definitely about doing things to be okay *before* we feel good. To send our brain the activation signals it needs. **It means to sustain the idea that as we move, the path will appear....**

The idea is not to smile foolishly while, inside, we have a heavy soul; instead, it implies adopting a proactive attitude that includes leaving the sofa and the house, doing sports and calling friends and/or family, looking for things that make us smile despite the pain. All this is without waiting to have the strength to do it because precisely by doing so, our brain gives us the power we need.

Marta is a 69-year-old lady, had been widowed a year and a half before and still in mourning, "As it is appropriate".

She came to me because she couldn't cope with sadness.

She described to me how difficult it had been to cope with her husband's illness. Above all, she explained to me how difficult it was to get ahead on her own after 43 years of marriage.

I asked her about her daily activities, and she replied, "Not much... I just don't feel like it. My friends tell me it's normal and that in time I may get over it. Or not..."

I worked with her to emphasize the need to take her life into her own hands and not to adopt a passive attitude as time continues to pass by. Considering herself as a victim was something that not only had weakened her situation but threatened to trigger a chronic sadness.

We also talked about cultural and social factors and about how our entourage (family/neighbors), although it may have good intentions, is not always the best counselor.

We made a "proactive list" with Marta; we wrote down on paper an inventory of things that she could do that would give her pleasure and, at the same time, prevent her from stagnation.

It was not an easy journey at first, but little by little she gained in confidence and enthusiasm: "I always wanted to learn how to paint, but I never had time, and now I could take free classes at the town hall," she said. "Sometimes, I feel like going for a walk, but I don't know ... what are they going to think about me... having been widowed so recently...".

The list was a resounding success for Marta. After a few more consultations, she began to dress in more vivid colors; even her expression and posture changed. She found her vocation in painting and started making plans to exhibit in a contest at the town hall. Since she lived in a small village, there were again cultural factors: Some of the neighbors scrutinized her with *reprehending glances. Marta no longer* paid attention to *them.*

The most striking thing was that the point on the list that cost the least was the one that brought the most benefits: Smile.

We had agreed to smile at least ten times a day. At first, she felt strange and judged, but after a few days, she no longer had to force it; the smile came by itself. Marta didn't need anti-depression medication, just some anxiolytic pills to help her sleep, which we stopped within a few months. Her positive predisposition and **refusal to adopt a self-indulgent** *attitude (sometimes socially accepted and encouraged by others) helped her to take control of her situation. She recognized bereavement as a natural process, which is necessary to go through until a new meaning is found in life. This process is not necessarily treated with pills; in fact, it rarely is. Instead, it requires a proactive attitude, reflection, and,* **above all, moving towards improvement and not waiting for it to come.**

6. Understand that the problem is not what happens to us, but our interpretation of what happens to us

We are not disturbed by what happens to us, but by our thoughts about what happens to us.
-Epictetus, 1st century B.C.

There is nothing either good or bad, but thinking makes it so.
-William Shakespeare, *Hamlet*, Act 2, Scene 2.

The one thing you can't take away from me is the way I choose to respond to what you do to me. The last of one's freedoms is to choose one's attitude in any given circumstance.
-Viktor E. Frankl

There is a popular saying: "Life is ten percent what happens to you and ninety percent how you react to it." In life, attitude is almost everything; it is what shapes our beliefs and desires. Setbacks, and even tragedies, can occur throughout our lives, but it is up to us to interpret them. It is essential to know that we can remain in control of emotions in any given situation.

The circumstances and facts of our lives provoke thoughts, and these thoughts provoke emotions, which determine our character:

Facts > thoughts > emotions > character.

In this chain, what we can change is the thoughts and what they trigger.

Indeed, **we can choose what we think. The facts, for better or worse, are unchangeable.**

Here is a practical example: If I am suspended from three classes in school, I can choose to think that this is a catastrophe. I can select the thought that I will never be able to overcome this, and that my life is destined to fail. Or I can decide that I will believe that this is not that big a deal, that I've come out of other difficult situations, and that with a little support, I'll get ahead.

Both statements may be valid, but the emotions that provoke each will be very different.

These irrational beliefs ("my life is destined to fail") are unproductive and bring a high emotional cost.

So why not choose to think of something that brings us well-being and peace of mind?

Many people blame their circumstances on their mishaps and, as a result, they do nothing to change. In their minds, nothing depends on them, and they feel at the mercy of events. They believe that an event is equivalent to its outcome; however, for the mentally productive person, adversity is an opportunity to thrive.

What allows the latter person to get ahead? They understand that what matters is not what has happened to them in their lives, but how they react to it. The way a person decides to respond to events is what will shape their feelings, actions, and results.

We carry within us the emotional elements we need to get ahead; but sometimes, we need to discover them.

As the American painter and writer Walter Anderson once wrote:

"I am responsible. Although I may not be able to prevent the worst from happening, I am responsible for my attitude toward the inevitable misfortunes that darken life. Bad things do happen; how I respond to them defines my character and the quality of my life. I can choose to sit in perpetual sadness, immobilized by the gravity of my loss, or I can choose to rise from the pain and treasure the most precious gift I have—life itself."

Adversity is something we all face at some point in our lives. However, we are not defined by these circumstances but by the way we react to them. That's what reveals our real character.

Knowledge is gained from everything we do and everything that happens to us. We learn valuable lessons over time based on our repeated experiences and the ways in which we react to them. Every difficulty can present an opportunity. We just need to recognize that instead of adopting a defeatist approach. Our thoughts and attitudes mold and shape our lives.

Everyone has a choice when it comes to their reactions, although, if we tend to follow an unhealthy habit like getting angry or depressed, we need to remember that such an approach leads us nowhere. We need to try a different method. We should do it consistently and with discipline, almost with a sporting spirit, practicing mental gymnastics that will soon pay off.

The more I live and experience, the more I realize the impact of my attitude towards life. Attitude, in my opinion, is more important than facts. It's more important than the past, education, money, circumstances, failure, success, or what other people think, say, or do. It's more important than appearance or talent. It can produce prosperity or ruin governments, companies, even homes.

The most notable thing is that, except in cases of deep depression or other severe psychiatric pathology, we can determine, every day, the attitude we will adopt. **We can choose every single day of our lives to be happy no matter what happens.**

We can't change our past. We can't alter the fact that people will act a certain way. **We can't modify the inevitable. All we can do is control what's up to us: our attitude.** I am therefore convinced that life is ten percent of what happens to us and that the other ninety percent is how we react. And that applies to everyone. We are in charge of our attitudes. We are, as Nelson Mandela said, "the captains of our destiny."

How we react to everything that happens around us can then determine the quality of our lives. As we said, there are things in our world that we can control and others that we cannot; it is essential to accept this. As soon as this knowledge moves to a conscious plane, we can begin to feel and develop a greater sense of mastery in life.

It is that sense of control and stability that could help prevent some of the depression and anxiety cases that today form part of mental health consultation waiting lists.

Gradually, society has been losing its ability to deal with incertitude and has become increasingly dependent on a world where the absence of certainty is more the rule than the exception.

One easy solution seems to be antidepressants and anxiolytics; the path of self-knowledge, though, while long and arduous, is the one that can bring the most significant benefits in the medium and long term.

Adrián is a 35-year-old architect. He first came to my office with a case of depression in the context of separation and job loss.

His girlfriend had left him after a five-year-long relationship, right after he was fired from his job at a major architectural firm.

During our first few sessions, Adrián told me about the pain caused by his broken relationship, his feeling of loneliness, and his perception that he was a failure while most of his friends were married and had children.

Added to this was his feeling of humiliation for being dismissed, and wondering why this had happened to him. He had worked hard for the company, even though he did not always find himself at ease or feel well treated. He struggled to assimilate the fact that the company did not need him anymore. This generated anger and frustration, damaging an already battered ego.

In his words, Adrián felt "cursed,". The anger of being "excluded" from this world added up to his understandable sadness.

We started working on realizing the positive side of the situation. Once his breakup pain had subsided, Adrián came to realize that, in reality, his relationship had been going nowhere, as he and his girlfriend did not share the same values. Although they loved each other, their goals did not coincide (she wanted to have children, while he was not very convinced, for example). He started accepting that sometimes love is not enough, and that it takes many more things for a partnership to thrive. He ended up admitting that breaking up their relationship, perhaps, had not been such a bad decision.

As for his work, he gradually recognized that despite the high salary and status that came with it, he had felt frustrated and restricted in his creativity while working there. Sometimes he blamed himself because he had resigned his ideals in return for the comfort it gave him to pay his mortgage.

He was discharged after a few months, and a year later, he called me to say hello.

He told me he had used his savings to create an architecture studio specializing in social housing designs that worked with NGOs. He was earning just enough to live, but he was genuinely proud, and his quality of life had improved.

Feeling so good about himself had attracted the right person to his life. He had met Isabel, a social worker who was collaborating with him on one of his projects; they were expecting a child and planning to get married.

Adrián said goodbye with a phrase that summed up the whole therapeutic process. He told me that his suffering had come from his distorted outlook on life before it all happened. "In the end," he said, "what I considered to be a calamity was the best thing that could ever happen to me..."

In short: Emotions arise from specific thoughts. We must learn to think more productively. The most common irrational thinking is to take everything too seriously and anticipate misfortunes. **Irrational beliefs are false, unproductive, and cause suffering. Getting rid of such beliefs isn't easy, but it's absolutely worth it.**

7. Abandon the unbridled pursuit of success

Success follows doing what you want to do. There is no other way to be successful.
-Malcolm Forbes

There are many definitions for success, some more accurate than others. The most common one has to do with an image or a stereotype. It is thought that the successful person is the one who possesses the complete combo: physical beauty, a sophisticated lifestyle, luxury houses, and expensive cars.

Advertisers use that image to sell us all kinds of products. **This is a concept that many people adopt: an idea of success that requires external validation. For them, success is getting what one wants, as opposed to the budist notion of happiness that implies wanting what one gets.**

Indeed, many people confuse success with wealth, which in turn has several aspects. Some try to accumulate many things, many of them worthless. Others just like to see their bank accounts grow bigger. Is this the sensible path?

Money, fame, power, wealth, championships are only by-products. This goes hand in hand with what Warren Buffett says, *"Making money isn't the backbone of our guiding purpose; making money is the by-product of our guiding purpose. If you're doing something you love, you're more likely to put your all into it, and that generally equates to making money."*

According to a joint study from Northwestern University and the University of Massachusetts titled *"Lottery Winners and Accident Victims: Is Happiness Relative?"*[2], after a year, one can compare the mood of those who became millionaires and those who suffer a mishap.

The study found that lottery winners were more likely to end up unhappy because many of them ended up losing everything.

Research from the universities of Kentucky, Pittsburg, and Vanderbilt found that those who pocketed between 39,000 and 118,000 euros through gambling ended up ruined within 3 to 5 years.

Studies suggest that nearly 80% of game-of-chance-winning millionaires squander their fortunes in less than a decade.

Money is only necessary to a certain extent; if we have our basic needs met, we can consider ourselves fortunate.

According to a study conducted by Purdue University and published in the journal *Nature Human Behavior* [3], happiness does come at a price, and this price varies from one continent to another.

This research used data from the *Gallup World Poll*, a survey of more than 1.7 million people in 164 different countries. The cost of living in each region was taken into account to reach the first conclusion: the average income needed to be happy is around USD 75 thousand per person per year. In the case of Latin America, an annual income of USD 35 thousand per capita is required. According to the research, earning more than USD 95 thousand per year can have negative effects.

Apparently, material dissatisfaction can occur when there is a tendency to compare ourselves with those of higher social strata because we invariably end up losing. The more we have, the more the standard of living increases, the more we get used to a lifestyle that forces us to maintain or increase our level of income.

It is also apparent from the study that, in some cases, more impoverished people and regions are considered happier (if happiness is a measurable value) than more developed societies.

The reason for this is probably that these less wealthy, happy individuals live in relative isolation and do not have the opportunity to compare – pointlessly – with others.

An entire book could be written about that propensity to look for more, to never have enough, to pursue the mirage of "when I change cars or buy that house or have that new cell phone, I will be happy." When we finally achieve this sort of happiness, it doesn't last for long: about three months, to be more accurate, according to studies.

The moral of the matter is that money should have its rightful place on our priority scale, as a means of achieving our goals.

Therefore, those who tend to think only in terms of money lose sight of the real value of life. Those who underestimate money's importance suffer the same fate.

Therefore, the following question arises: what is success?

The definition is very personal, but basically, the real idea of success should involve living as one wants while following one's principles. And to do that, you don't always need money or power. We will not always get what we want, a reality that will provide us with life lessons and make us learn. And learning is the reason we are here in this world.

Does living as you want mean doing whatever you want? Not at all. It means conducting yourself independently of external constraints that prevent you from achieving happiness, while always respecting the rights of others.

The definition of success may be different for everyone. For myself, achieving success means making a living out of my passion, having my basic needs met, and living in line with my values. Perhaps, for me, it also means leaving a legacy in terms of my philosophy of life (for example, by writing this book, whose publication alone is a success for me). However, it doesn't bother me too much either. My aim is to achieve these dreams, not random ones or those imposed by society (or my family or colleagues), but true ones, the ones that add value, those that thrill and fulfill me.

There are many stories of people who pursued a mistaken idea of what success is in search of power and money. Many of them found themselves feeling empty, their families broken, isolated, if not ruined financially. Some high-performance American athletes are a clear example of this, reflected in the excellent documentary "*Broke*".

The film mentions a 2009 Sports Illustrated magazine article (4), according to which 60 % of former NBA players are bankrupt within five years of retirement. 78% of former NFL players filed for bankruptcy or are in financial difficulty within two years after the end of their careers. Ravaged by bad investments, beset by lenders, besieged by injuries, and naturally prone to show off, many professional athletes are surprised by harsh economic realities after years of living a life of (relative) success.

A well-known singing teacher and talent scout once told me what she did during auditions to ascertain those children who would succeed: "In addition to talent, those who enjoy what they do generally succeed. They arrive smiling, and their faces show no tension. The others, those who come forced by their parents, those who come only in search of fame. . . even if they demonstrate some skill, they have less chance."

In this regard, in the highly acclaimed film *"Billy Elliot,"* we can find a good example: During one of the scenes, Billy has just danced superbly and stands before the directors of the Royal Ballet School in London, although his difficult character does not impress them much. When asked why he dances, his eyes light-up as he describes a "fire in the body" he feels when he does what he loves, casting aside his bad image and getting the scholarship that means the starting point of a successful career in ballet.

Success in life can mean, for others, having the opportunity to meet all our personal needs, whether financial or not. It means being able to feed ourselves, dress ourselves, and have a home to go back to every night. Get medical attention if necessary. To laugh and have fun with our friends. To love and be loved. To have a good job that we enjoy. To get your own and others' recognition. To do what we are passionate about, something that makes us lose track of time, something we would actually pay to do.

That's why it's so important to be clear about our priorities, to know what is really important to us and what we want to achieve in life. Sadly, many people don't know them.

Few people know how to value what they have and what they have been able to achieve. Those who take care of their things and care about their future and the real well-being of themselves and their families are the ones who know that succeeding does not depend on the goods they have or the money they earn, but on how they use these to meet their needs and aspirations.

Martin is a 45-year-old lawyer and a member of a prominent family, which was a great help in achieving social positions and employment.

He came to my office with a mood disorder and an alcohol problem.

Basically, Martin had not found meaning in his life. He had gone a long way in his profession and had raised a family, but something was missing.

He had no idea what was happening to him. "I have a perfect life; I don't lack anything ... But I'm bored. I dislike everything ... despite being a person who has it all..."

We start by subtly questioning his idea of success. Could he consider himself really successful when his career was imposed by his family?

Could he truly love a job that he picked because of his family's contacts?

How did he feel about having a boss (his father-in-law) above him giving orders that didn't always fit his principles?

We started exploring options and using his creativity. I suggested him to imagine what his ideal life would be like, which job would he pick if his economic needs were met (and in his case they were).

He told me he always liked to cook. He was happy in the kitchen. He spent hours in there preparing meals for family and friends.

He struggled to arrive at that conclusion because, for him, cooking was a natural gift; it was so easy; he had never thought he could make a living out of it.

Within a few months, Martin set up a food truck where he sold a small but satisfactory and high-quality menu.

Success (the real kind) took little time to arrive: People appreciated his work, he had more hours off and a better quality of life, and despite earning less than in his previous work, he had a feeling of fulfillment...

In conclusion:

Perhaps we should stop expending energy to seek success in the traditional sense. Maybe we should invest in finding something or someone that gives meaning to our lives.

Success is peace of mind that is the direct result of self-satisfaction in knowing you did your best to become the best that you are capable of becoming. Furthermore, only one person can ultimately judge the level of your success: you.

The real challenge, of course, is striving to reach your personal best, and that is totally under your control. When you achieve that, you have achieved success. Period! You are a winner and only you fully know if you won.

If you are striving to become the best version of yourself, you are a success.

8. Understand that happiness is not the absence of problems

Think logically, and you have a chance to solve a problem. Reacting emotionally to it prolongs and worsens your dilemma.
— **Stewart Stafford**

Many people suffer from *"low frustration tolerance"*, or *"short-term hedonism."* This concept describes an inability to tolerate unpleasant feelings or stressful situations. It stems from believing that reality should be as wished for, and that any frustration should be resolved quickly and easily. People with low frustration tolerance experience emotional disturbance when failures are not resolved rapidly. Behaviors are then directed towards avoiding frustrating events, but, paradoxically, this leads to increased frustration and even more mental stress.

Frustration is inevitable for all of us. Without the emotional and mental resources required to manage the problems of daily life, disappointment and sadness await us.

Problems do not necessarily create a difficult and miserable life. In fact, whether something is truly a problem is mostly a matter of perspective. Often, though, people are defeated by problems, succumbing to feelings of anger, fear, and anxiety.

On the other hand, some people succeed despite difficulties. They are able to handle or solve problems when they arise. They do not allow negative emotions to interfere with their ability to think about solutions and take the next step.

Instead of asking "Why me?", they ask themselves, "How do I solve it, and what do I have to learn from this?" Our attitude influences the actions we take in response to problems and, in many cases, determines the outcome. Consciously deciding what approach to take to each situation is important, especially if we regard that situation as adverse.

If, instead of considering that "fate" is conspiring against us, we choose to accept and conquer the challenges that life presents, we will move significantly toward success and happiness, even more so if we appreciate the opportunity it gives us to succeed.

It is normal to feel overwhelmed, helpless, and impotent at times, and it is right at the level of our sentiments that we must begin to work.

Sometimes, life closes certain doors and it's time to move on. That's fine, because we risk stagnating if circumstances don't force us to keep moving. Many of us are passive by nature; if issues didn't arise, we would do nothing to initiate change. In this sense, some complications are eventually revealed as true blessings.

We tend to forget that complicated problems or situations can end up being beneficial. A classic example is that of the enraged traveler who misses his flight by a few minutes, only to read in the newspaper the next day that his plane had an accident.

And how about that breakup that brought us great sadness at the time, but in the end, we thank God for having ended the relationship since it allowed us to meet our current partner? Or that mediocre job that we were fired from, thanks to which we found the career of our dreams?

Patience is not waiting for problems to disappear; it is maintaining the right attitude while working to resolve them, knowing that the effort is worthwhile and that there is a lesson to learn in the process—and that every step forward will make us feel better than anything we can imagine. **We realize that the struggle is not on the way, but is the way itself.**

Isabel, 49, felt that the sky had fallen on her head the day she first came to see me.

Financial problems had coincided with her daughter's recent diagnosis of breast cancer. Also, her youngest son had failed his university access exam, momentarily halting his dream of becoming a lawyer. To make things worse, she had been fired from the hotel where she worked as a cook and to which she had dedicated her life, even at the cost of taking time away from her family!

She kept wondering why so many calamities had befallen her. Her sadness was compounded by an angry feeling of injustice.

Through therapy, we changed the approach of helplessness to the avatars of fate to a position of empowerment. Isabel began to wonder what she could learn from this situation, in spite of the pain and uncertainty. In time, her daughter's health improved, and the disease process brought them closer than ever. After being fired, she had lots of free time; this allowed her to strengthen her relationship with her youngest son. She realized that, in reality, her previous employment not only took away quality time to spend with her family, but she did not feel appreciated. Over time she set up a small bakery with her children, which is gradually thriving.

The road is not problem-free, but Isabel faces adverse situations differently. And sometimes she even thanks them.

51

9. Accept

God, grant me the serenity to accept the things I cannot change, Courage to change the things I can, and wisdom to know the difference.

-Reinhold Niebuhr

Of course, there is no formula for success, except perhaps an unconditional acceptance of life, and what it brings.

-Arthur Rubinstein

Accepting leads to serenity and harmony. **Accepting a problem is the beginning of solving it.** Accepting a disease may be the beginning of curing it.

"What you resist, persists." This quote, attributed to Swiss psychiatrist Carl Gustav Jung, encapsulates the central idea of this chapter. And we could add: "What you acccpt, gcts transformed."

Sometimes, you observe others' lives and you think you will never experience what other people are experiencing, whether positive or negative. We believe it's never going to happen to us. But the true beauty of life is that it is unpredictable. Nothing is permanent; everything changes. Many things can happen that will transform us and have an impact on our lives. The problem is that we need to cultivate the ability to accept what happens and truly embrace it.

We need to develop a habit of looking through a positive mindset rather than using a negative, more defeatist approach.

Life will bring many challenges, such as the death of a loved one or being fired from a job and it's not easy to accept a setback when we're suffering. We wish those things would have never happened. But if we start building up acceptance, we can look at the future with a different perspective. We can learn to accept, instead of resisting and fighting unproductively.

We should try to embrace what happens to us because if we fight and resist, we generate exhausting mental turbulence, which sometimes leads to mood disorders and anxiety.

We might want things to be different in the future, but in the present moment, we need to take things as they are. This is how we can make life flow smoothly.

Yes, acceptance is a choice. Challenging, no doubt about it, But nevertheless a choice.

Whether it's a personal loss, a wasted opportunity, or a sudden change in our plans, being able to accept things beyond our control will help us maintain internal peace and happiness.

Acceptance, in my opinion, is the key to turning our life from form a bunch of random momentary moments of bliss into lasting happiness. It gives us a sense of control in our lives. Acceptance allows us to set aside feelings of helplessness in the face of the chaos caused by anxiety and hopelessness.

Practicing acceptance helps us to live serenely despite never knowing what will happen next. Acceptance is a good shield against life avatars.

Acceptance has nothing to do with weakness, and it is not a synonym for conformity or mediocrity. Still, we need to learn how to identify when it's time to persist and when it's time to accept.

One way to make acceptance more comfortable is to list all possible explanations for what we are experiencing.

For example, we needed to have that job that we were fired from in order to explore other options that would satisfy us more. We needed to overcome that toxic relationship to grow and move forward in life.

Finding the lesson or purpose behind each challenge will help us accept it rather than fight it. We can choose not to judge what happens to us. Furthermore, we can choose to believe that everything happens for a reason, and that gentler winds will always blow. That is the beginning of true acceptance.

Sometimes accepting also means giving up searching obsessively for meaning in what happens to us.

Maybe the important thing is not to understand why something happened. Sometimes we don't need to understand to move on with our life.

In other words: When the unexpected happens, instead of complaining and overthinking, we should choose to live with it.

More straightforward still: If we can't change the wind direction, let's adjust the sails.

Once upon a time, after years of training, a mountaineer began his journey with the firm intention of conquering a very high mountain.

It was getting late, but he decided to continue the ascent.

The night came quickly, and visibility dropped to zero. Everything was black; clouds covered the moon and the stars.

Climbing up a cliff, just a few feet from the top, he slipped and began to slide, falling dizzyingly. The man could do nothing. He kept falling, trying to hold on to any rock or ledge.

He started feeling the nearness of death when he suddenly felt the fierce pull of the rope that tied him from the waist to the stakes nailed to the mountain wall.

In that moment of stillness, suspended in the air, he could only shout: HELP ME! SOMEBODY HELP ME!

Out of nowhere, a grave, deep voice answered him:

- WHAT DO YOU WANT ME TO DO?

– Save me, PLEASE!

– DO YOU REALLY THINK I CAN SAVE YOU?

– Of course, I do!

– THEN CUT THE STRING THAT HOLDS YOU...

There was a moment of silence. The man clung even tighter to the rope.

The next day, the rescue team found him hanging dead. Frozen, clinging tightly to the rope... a meter and a half above the ground.

Acceptance, as we see, is closely related to the concept of "letting go" and going with the flow. It is not part of our standard skills set when we are born. It often takes time, sometimes a lifetime, to learn.

10. Take one step at a time

When you improve a little each day, eventually big things occur.... Not tomorrow, not the next day, but eventually, a big gain is made. Don't look for the big, quick improvement. Seek the small improvement one day at a time. That's the only way it happens — and when it happens, it lasts.
– John Wooden, NBA coach

"One step at a time." We've all heard this expression before. This concept is crucial in any improvement process. When starting something new, it is not possible to do everything all at once. It is advisable to go gradually, doing one thing at a time. If we start going to the gym, we can't make a week's worth of progress in one session. The same applies if we want to get rid of a persistent bad habit. Over time, through consistency, results will appear and will produce an unmistakable sense of satisfaction. These little joys are the basis for acquiring the necessary consistency that allows us to persist. If we try to do a lot of things at once and put ourselves under too much pressure, we will feel overwhelmed. We will lose sight of the target, and our goals will become uncertain and unattainable.

Taoism is a religious philosophy practiced mostly in Japan, and it can be credited with the extraordinary resilience and recovery capabilities of the Japanese people.

The exciting thing about this approach to life is that it invites us to propose very small goals so that failing becomes practically impossible. Part of the philosophy claims that if we improve a tiny aspect of our life every day, over the medium and long term we will achieve a significant transformation. The idea is that it is smarter to make small but continuous improvements, rather than strive for large transformations that are unachievable precisely because of their size.

This is a very useful approach that addresses two significant obstacles to progress. The first of them is the fear of change. As the proposal is not to make major changes, anxiety decreases. More realistic expectations are set, and therefore fewer disappointments are experienced.

The second problem this philosophy addresses is that it helps to prevent us from procrastinating; that is, from postponing change indefinitely. If we feel that we have a gigantic mission to achieve, we often defer starting on it. This is because we think that such a significant task will demand so much from us, it becomes intimidating. This method of continuous tiny improvements eliminates that factor.

We need to appreciate and be proud of those small achievements, and then feel even more satisfied when we look back and see how all those little actions led to a wonderful result. If we do not praise ourselves throughout our journey, we will lose all motivation before achieving our goals. We need to make sure we encourage ourselves from time to time.

We must not allow ourselves to become discouraged, no matter how long the road is. **The idea is not that the first step takes us where we want to go, but that it moves us forward from where we are.**

And if the way is still not clear from our viewpoint... that's another reason for moving on!

Andrea was overwhelmed by her new job, so much so that she was thinking of asking for a leave due to anxiety.

As an employee of an advertising agency, she was responsible for the executive management of advertising campaigns, something she had never done before.

Her strength was creativity, not so much organization or management.

The enormity of the task overwhelmed and paralyzed her.

They had thrown her in at the deep end, and it was a matter of swimming or sinking. And she felt that she was sinking.

In therapy, we started working on organization skills, a concept she was not familiar with.

We adopted a simple strategy:

1) Write down the desired results.

2) Note the main steps that must be taken in order to attain that result.

3) Divide those steps into smaller, more easily achieved stages.

4) Set some timeframes by which these smaller steps need to be ready, and then start to work on them, keeping these deadlines in mind (yes, one step at a time).

The trick is to divide a big task into smaller steps that are easier to understand and handle. Also, to ask for help if necessary. There's no point in exhausting yourself if you can delegate some of the tasks.

The plan worked, and Andrea understood that, with time and patience, she could apply it to every area of her life.

11. Develop an abundance mindset

Both abundance and lack exist simultaneously in our lives, as parallel realities. It is always our conscious choice which secret garden we will tend... when we choose not to focus on what is missing from our lives but are grateful for the abundance that's present— love, health, family, friends, work, the joys of nature and personal pursuits that bring us pleasure—the wasteland of illusion falls away and we experience Heaven on earth.

-Sarah Ban Breathnach

People, in a very general way, are one of two types: those focused on scarcity and those focused on abundance.

When we sustain a scarcity mentality, we tend to adopt certain behaviors that, in the short term, help manage the lack of something, but in the long run, only make things worse.

A book entitled Scarcity (5), (Mullainathan & Eldar 2013) discusses the concept of scarcity through the following questions: What happens in our minds when we feel we have very little? How does the context of lack determine our choices and behaviors? Scarcity is seen not as just a physical, palpable limitation. Scarcity affects our thinking and feeling; it automatically and powerfully orients the mind to unmet needs.

The context of scarcity, therefore, can make us short-sighted (which, in statistics, is called biased). When our mind is focused on the present hardship, we tend to attract even more scarcity, and we detract from the possibility of thinking big, of expanding our limits, of going further... It is the opposite of focusing on abundance, on opportunities, on "Why not?"

A perspective of abundance tends to lead to healthier and more productive behavior.

Let's look at the characteristics of both approaches.

1. Risk taking vs. fearfulness

Those who focus on scarcity remain too much within their comfort zone. These people believe that there is never enough resources. Still, they are not willing to look beyond their comfort zones to find more opportunities. While audacity isn't always a good approach, being willing to get out of your comfort zone can be worthwhile. This can be profitable in certain areas of life such as relationships, work, travel, and daily experiences.

Those with an abundance-oriented mindset, on the other hand, believe that many potential directions are available, whether in the workplace or personally. People who have this view tend to be more creative and more prone to personal growth. They thrive and have a broader picture of life in general, which allows them to get on with living instead of getting stuck in the same place because they don't see opportunities or are too scared to go after them. Of course, they tend to have their own comfort zones, but they are more than happy to step out of them when necessary.

2. Generosity vs. meanness

Those who have a scarcity mentality feel that resources such as money, time, and success are limited. This leads to a potentially harmful, misunderstood over competitiveness. These people fear that there is not enough of these resources for everyone, that they must fight to achieve. They find it difficult to "let go" and share, to demonstrate the behavior that makes things more comfortable in work, friendships, and relationships.

Those who profess a mindset of abundance see precisely that: plenty. There's enough for everyone, and there always will be. This does not mean that competitiveness is not a good thing; it just means that things can be approached with a healthier attitude. Instead of pushing everyone aside to grab the front row seat of life, these individuals recognize that a full row of seats is available to them and to others as well.

This viewpoint allows for a more fulfilling, productive life.

3. Team work vs. competitiveness

The way we feel about sharing is closely related to our outlook. Some people have doubts about sharing ideas at work, for example, for fear that they will not be credited or rewarded if someone else " steals" their idea. This is understandable, but it can also project an image of selfishness.

This type of conduct also massively influences relationships: if you are always hiding something, if you are distrusting, there is no way to get the intimacy and complicity needed for a partnership to thrive.

Instead of seeing genuine connections as satisfying, some people may see them as potential threats to their future success and a waste of their current resources.

One thing that can clear our path in life is our ability and willingness to share. Success is not always the result of individual efforts!

Being comfortable sharing ideas without being threatened or intimidated is essential in most aspects of life. This type of behavior leads to healthier choices and favors more productive environments, and it facilitates relationships of all kinds.

Practicing generosity is a positive way to live life. It brings benefits, whether it's helping with charity work, forging close relationships with people, or simply being more open.

Even when feeling depressed, the message we send to our brain through our acts of generosity is "I have a lot to give." In some cases, it works true miracles as far as mental health recovery is concerned. In fact, I usually recommend volunteering to my patients as it can be very therapeutic.

4. Confidence vs. fear

The scarcity frame of reference is driven by fear. It is concerned about the lack of time and believes the resources for which we need to battle are limited.

This type of posture tends to isolate people, which confirms their distorted, pessimistic concept of the world.

Being battered by negative thoughts and emotions tends to end in defeat and frustration. Even if these people succeed in a material sense, they may fear losing everything, so they rarely really enjoy what they have and can only covet more of everything.

The scarcity mentality will see any setbacks as a major flop, fueling their fears of not succeeding (or losing what they have), keeping them trapped in a cycle of defeatism.

At the opposite end of the spectrum, the mindset of abundance is driven by an attitude of general enjoyment and greater confidence in future success.

This belief, which is certainly comparable to the faith promulgated by various religions, is based on the fact that there will always be many opportunities. This attitude helps hopeful people when they suffer some setbacks, as they know they will have a better chance of succeeding.

5. Optimism vs. Negativity

People with a scarcity mentality tend to have their beliefs firmly rooted in a sea of negativity, which is harmful in many ways. As we have mentioned, this can significantly affect work and relationships. For them, nothing is enough, there is never enough available for them, and they can't see any way to increase the possibilities on their horizon. This creates a cycle of negativity that continues to strengthen over time. With their focus on what they don't have and what is lacking in their lives, they often feel too exhausted to pursue the achievement of their goals.

This kind of mentality often formulates **self-fulfilling prophecies**; this concept refers to the socio-psychological phenomenon of someone "predicting" or expecting something, and this "prediction" or expectation comes true simply because one *believes* it will, and their resulting behaviors align to fulfil those beliefs. This suggests peoples' beliefs influence their actions. The principle behind this phenomenon is people create consequences regarding people or events, based on their previous knowledge toward that specific subject.

If this sounds familiar, it may be time time to make changes before we get too stuck to move forward in our lives.

The abundance-oriented mentality is a positive place to be, although this does not mean that everyone who adopts this approach is always happy and satisfied! Of course, there are rejections and mishaps along the way, but it's the way that people deal with these circumstances that helps them move forward.

Instead of getting caught up in a downward spiral, optimistic people are confident that something else will always turn up, whether it's a new partner, a better job, or another opportunity. This attitude is what allows them to grow and succeed, as they can focus on future opportunities while learning from past mistakes.

Clara, 39, decided to start therapy because her life was "stagnant."

Recently divorced, she couldn't find a way to improve her meager income.

"I feel that life is a complicated game, and I don't get the rules. I just don't understand them," she said with discouragement. She compared herself to her friends, who exhibited via social media a life of apparent happiness.

We started working on her fears, the idea that she was not prepared to play this game, that in this world there is not enough for everyone, and it was up to her to deal with it. We analyzed her strengths and the reasons she didn't take more risks to get better results.

We made a list of possibilities, no matter how crazy they might seem. One of them was to stand in a corner with a sign that said, "I'm looking for a boyfriend and a well-paid job," an idea which produced hilarity, although it also left her pensive.

The aim was to stimulate the creativity that Clara had dormant within herself, to enhance a proactive attitude and change the vital approach to scarcity.

Over time, two changes occurred:

She began advertising with relative success on a rural tourism site her nearly abandoned family home, which she reconditioned with her savings. This eventually gave her a certain economic relief, but above all, it gave her immense personal satisfaction.

She felt that she had "created something out of nothing," in her words.

The second thing that changed was her emotional life. During therapy, we had come to the conclusion that she did not need someone by her side to feel complete, but she decided to take her "proactive attitude "a little bit further. She signed up for an app to find a boyfriend. This was something unthinkable for her according to her own vital codes of scarcity.

Not long after she moved in with Ernesto, a mechanic who had signed up even though he didn't believe much in social media either because, he said, "It's full of nutty people."

12. Admit your limitations and set up realistic goals

A goal properly set is halfway reached.

-Zig Ziglar

A certain kind of "self-help" literature has done a lot of damage to those who it pretended to want to help.

Numerous authors declare that we can achieve anything we want—if we want it with all our strength. Unfortunately, that is not the case: It is a big lie. It is not only a fallacy, but it also makes us feel guilty, because it insinuates that if we don't get something it is because we haven't desired it enough or didn't believe in our dreams as much as we should have...

Accepting our limitations can be liberating. Accepting our limitations does not mean resigning and surrendering. On the contrary, it means, "I can't do this right now, but this is something I'll work to learn about, or I'll devote myself to."

It is perfectly valid to reach out to our dreams. Still, **when perseverance turns into stubbornness, it is no longer a virtue....**

We can pursue our dreams, but our happiness and well-being should not depend on achieving them because the attainment of our dreams is not always up to us.

As hard as it may seem, it's unrealistic to say that we can always achieve whatever we want.

Everyone has limitations. **Can every high school basketball player become Michael Jordan? Is it helpful to pursue a dream, systematically ignoring that we are actually equipped for another kind of greatness?** Genes, social circumstances, and countless other factors beyond our control limit how far we can go in each case. We need to take stock of our talents and examine our weakest areas as well.

We know that something is unrealistic when, despite our sincere persistence, the result is, at best, mediocre.

When we insist on trying for something without getting the results we were aiming for, we should ask ourselves whether we really wanted to achieve it. Were we fighting for an unrealizable dream—or worse, one imposed by society or our environment? The energy we invest in an unobtainable dream could well be geared towards achieving what we are really destined for.

If, during the fight, we feel uncomfortable—chronically frustrated rather than enjoying it—that discomfort can be a sign that we are not doing what we should be doing. We are not fighting for the right cause or chasing the right dream.

Daniel, 35, had a motto: "Aim for the stars."

An enthusiastic singer, he was so passionate about music that he didn't stop to contemplate that he had had little success in finding the professional work he strived to. His ambitions were beyond his real abilities, and he often felt disappointed that all his efforts had not yet been rewarded. He felt discouraged, empty, and useless.

One day, he decided to accept the situation. He had an idea. He thought he could use the knowledge and experience acquired throughout his career to become an artist manager. A successful one, indeed. He understood that he was gifted for business and he started enjoying it. Over time, by investing his energy in developing his real talent, he achieved the success he hadn't managed to find as a singer.

Economic independence allowed him to start up a band consisting of friends that played in bars to "get a fix of music," as he likes to say. He even built a recording studio at home, where he edits albums for pleasure that no one buys, but that makes him very happy.

The last time he came to a consultation, I suggested that he make a synthesis of the process that led him to feel better. What he told me was revealing:

"As a child, I saw tall people, and I looked short, but I was underestimating my natural charm. When I was at school, I saw handsome classmates and found myself unattractive, but I forgot that my forte was using my intellect. I looked at others who were good at drawing, and I struggled with my pencil, undervaluing my talent at math.

"When I grew up, I saw people who easily found a partner and I found myself alone, disdaining the virtues of solitude and freedom. And so on. My limitations were endless.

"I wanted to stand out in something, and I chose music. I decided that it would be my dream, regardless of my lack of a natural talent for music.

"When I played, I saw colleagues who were successful. Me, I paddled against the current. I saw people enjoying themselves, and I saw myself working towards an impossible dream.

"But gradually, I have learned to live in peace with my limitations. I've noticed that:

-We all have limitations.

-Limitations have their own boundaries. When you change a little in space or time, limitations disappear.

-My weaknesses are a way to keep me under control.

-If I focus on my strengths, I go further than if I center on my limitations.

-My dream wasn't really to be a successful singer; my dream was to be able to live in a way that would allow me to continue making the music I love, even if very few went to my shows."

It is vital to have high hopes… as long as they are realistic. That doesn't mean we shouldn't set ambitious goals for ourselves or settle for less than we want, of course, but being honest about what's truly possible is also important.

We should say to ourselves: "If a target is within my reach, I will do everything I can to achieve it. But if the tension is excessive, I may have to adjust my aspirations." **Unrealistic expectations often foretell a disaster!**

And worse: Maybe they will distract us from our true destiny.

13. Prevent perfectionism from ruining your life

Understanding the difference between healthy striving and perfectionism is critical to laying down the shield and picking up your life. Research shows that perfectionism hampers success. In fact, it's often the path to depression, anxiety, addiction, and life paralysis.

— **Brené Brown, *The Gifts of Imperfection***

Beautiful things are never perfect.

— **Ancient Egyptian proverb**

Intuitively, we know that perfectionism is unrealistic and restrictive, a tyrant who takes us away from our goals. In fact, many experts emphasize the importance of making mistakes to create and accomplish great things.

Let's make it clear: it is laudable to tend to perfection, but when this avidity affects our daily life (paralyzing us, causing anxiety, stimulating obsessions, etc.), it ceases to be a virtue.

Perfectionism is a personality trait characterized by a person's eagerness for infallibility and setting high-performance standards, accompanied by critical self-assessments and concerns regarding the judgment of others . . . and of themselves.

Perfectionists tend to accept these distorted thoughts as if they were an unquestionable truth.

It is better to conceptualize perfectionism as a multidimensional feature, as psychologists agree that there are many positive and negative aspects. In its neurotic form, perfectionism drives people to try to achieve unattainable ideals or unrealistic goals, which often leads to depression and low self-esteem. On the contrary, adaptive perfectionism can motivate people to achieve their goals and gain pleasure in doing so.

Belen, a 30 years old novelist, was extremely insecure because she focused too much on her flaws.

She said to me during a session, "in one of my earliest memories, I am drawing. I don't remember what exactly, but I remember my mistakes. My pencil moved, trembling awkwardly, invading the margins. Instead of enjoying I used to get frustrated. The image disappeared long ago, but that feeling of profound failure, even of shame, has remained with me.

more often than I would like to admit, something seemingly unimportant will cause the same feeling to appear again. Something as trivial as accidentally crushing the pastries that my boyfriend's family brought for Christmas can remain in my mind for several days, accompanied by occasional self-reproach, wondering how could I be so stupid and telling myself I should have known better.

Not reaching a bigger goal, even when I know that achieving it would be almost impossible, can immediately bring me down. **Being a perfectionist has helped me obtain very specific standards and to become an overachiever in many ways. It has helped me do well in college, function well in my job, and is mainly the reason I excel in many personal aims and projects. Still, as I became an adult, I understood that perfectionism has some severe downsides.**

An editor once told me that he knew I was going to write a great book one day, but the particular project I had proposed to him did not fit the market; I felt defeated in a way that went beyond disappointment. The negative drowned out the positive. My inner voice told me I was never going to write a book because I was not good enough. That voice didn't care that this directly contradicted what the agent really wanted to state.

That's what perfectionism does. It does not discriminate; it is merciless. "

A recent meta-analysis made by Thomas Curran and Andrew Hill(6)was the first study to compare perfectionism between generations and goes from 1989 to 2016; it found significant increases of perfectionism among younger students in the United States, the United Kingdom, and Canada. In other words, 2016's average college student was much more likely to have perfectionist tendencies than students in the 1990s or early 2000's.

The increase in perfectionism does not mean that every generation feels more and more fulfilled. It likely means we're getting sicker, sadder, and even undermining our own potential.

 Perfectionism is ultimately a counterproductive way to move around the world. **It is based on an unbearable irony: Making and admitting mistakes is a necessary part of growing, learning, and actually being human.** It also makes us better in our careers and relationships and life in general. By avoiding mistakes at any cost, a perfectionist can make it harder to achieve your own goals.

But the drawback of perfectionism is not only that it prevents us from being the most successful version of ourselves. Perfectionist tendencies have been linked to a long list of clinical problems: Obsessive-compulsive disorders, depression, and anxiety (even in children), self-harm, social anxiety disorder and agoraphobia, eating disorders, chronic fatigue syndrome, insomnia, dyspepsia, chronic headaches and, most dangerous, even early mortality and suicide. It has also been shown that one of the most robust protection against anxiety and depression is self-pity (in a good way, without meaning we feel sorry for ourselves), something that perfectionists lack. And self-criticism, in which perfectionists are so good, predisposes to depression.

Culturally, we often see perfectionism as a positive thing. Even saying that you have perfectionist tendencies is exhibited as something to be proud of. It is another of so many maladaptive behaviors accepted and even encouraged by society.

Here is where perfectionism gets complicated and controversial. As we mentioned, we must differentiate between adaptive or "healthy" perfectionism (characterized by having high standards, motivation, and discipline) compared to a maladaptive or "unhealthy" version (when even the best never seems good enough and not meeting goals frustrates us).

Take, for example, that student who works hard and scores a low grade. If he tells himself: "I'm disappointed, but that's fine; I'm still a good person in general," that's healthy. If the message is: "I'm a mess. I'm not good enough," that's unhealthy perfectionism.

In the face of failure, perfectionists tend to respond more harshly in terms of emotions. They experience more guilt, more shame, and more anger. They give up more quickly. They have relatively obvious avoidance tendencies when things can't be perfect which is, in fact, most of the time.

That, of course, moves them away from the success they aspire to achieve.

The problem is, for perfectionists, performance is intertwined with their sense of self. **When they are unsuccessful, they are not only disappointed by how they did it, but they also feel shame for who they are.** Ironically, perfectionism is supposed to be a defense tactic to keep guilt at bay: **if you're perfect, you never fail, and if you never fail, there's no shame.**

The fear of failure as a form of perfectionism is also magnified in other ways. For example, on social media: make a mistake or slipup nowadays, and your fear of it expanding, even globally, may not be irrational.

Perfectionism is seen increasingly at younger ages. How can parents counter it? Perhaps by modeling and promoting healthy behaviors, observing their own perfectionist tendencies, displaying unconditional love and affection, and conveying responses like, "You really tried on that. I'm proud of the effort you put in." It is about creating an environment in which imperfection is not only accepted but also celebrated because it means that we are human. It's about increasing skills to tolerate the frustration that, like any other ability, can be exercised.

It is to set the idea that you do not have to be perfect to be loved.

How do we generate change? Probably by drawing upon kinder messages both to ourselves and others and by restraining ourselves consciously from overreacting to other people's mistakes and, above all, our own. Paradoxically, that includes trying not to criticize ourselves when we fail.

Like any other change at an emotional level, it's a full-time job. But we will probably feel freer and less stressed every time we replace criticism and perfectionism with compassion.

In conclusion:

1. Trust that it will all get done in time.

2. Question your inner judge and dispute negative outlooks.

3. Practice not judging others by your same standards.

4. Practice saying no more regularly.

5. Program pauses and recharge.

6. Create more pragmatic personal goals and expectations.

7. Bear in mind that time off is not time wasted.

8. Get away for a weekend holiday.

9. Stop misusing your time by multitasking.

10. Prioritize self-care and invest in yourself.

14. Don't be afraid of making mistakes

It is impossible to live without failing at something, unless you live so cautiously that you might as well not have lived at all—in which case, you fail by default.

—J.K. Rowling

This section, which is very much related to the previous one, is about people who do not necessarily seek perfection but are irrationally afraid to make mistakes.

In general, fears are influenced by our biological and genetic composition, as well as by our experiences.

We model our behavior according to what we see, much like children who absorb their parents' fears like sponges.

The messages we receive from others, including friends, coworkers, and the media, also play a role. We previously noted that constant pressure to improve performance could have the effect of triggering fears and making mistakes. Critical and ongoing judgments have a similar impact.

Having some fear of mistakes can be a good and adaptive thing; indeed, it can help improve performance. But excessive fear causes difficulties. Some people, for example, eat to avoid situations (meetings, appointments, presentations) that cause them anxiety. They fear making a mistake, and they may postpone a task because of the distress caused by the thought of being unable to complete it correctly. Others may spend hours reviewing their work to make sure it is error-free. In extreme cases this may manifest as OCD (obsessive-compulsive disorder).

Overcoming any fear involves confronting it directly. We need to allow ourselves to make little mistakes with unimportant consequences and motivate ourselves to set aside behaviors or security rituals.

Changing this thinking pattern is also vital, as are our conceptions—our interpretations—of events that happen around us and what is perpetuating them.

When we look at it another way, it's clear that we're not really afraid to *make* mistakes. What we actually fear is what we *believe* about making mistakes. That's what bothers us or causes us anxiety.

Sometimes we assume that making mistakes will lead to a terrible consequence that cannot be corrected or undone (such as being fired or ridiculed by others). Or we might believe that making mistakes is a sign of weakness or incompetence.

What's the best way to get rid of these ideas? Here are some helpful steps:

- identify the fear of error

- create a list of pros and cons of these thoughts and propose alternative ones

- choose a more realistic, useful, or productive way to perceive the situation

For example, let's look at a young man who feels embarrassed and anxious before stepping onstage to do karaoke when he is out with his friends. Initially, he believes that others will perceive him as clumsy and out of tune, and he won't be liked if he performs badly.

But then he activates the list of alternative thoughts: *People will not judge me based on this awkward situation; most of them are my friends, and they find me entertaining anyway. Besides, they are relaxed having fun, and everything's okay with them.*

By evaluating these thoughts, he realizes that his friends know him well, and although he is not a showman, the fact that they continue to invite him to these gatherings means they must enjoy his company.

It's important for this man to embrace this more realistic and useful perspective. He thinks: *Maybe I need to allow myself to make mistakes when I talk to other people. I don't judge other people when they say something unusual or uncomfortable to me. Maybe others aren't judging me when I make mistakes.*

Instead of always assuming that our thoughts are correct, we should question them, especially when they hurt us or cause anxiety.

It may seem that fear of making mistakes is unwavering. Fortunately, there are many practical and effective strategies for overcoming this fear. Still, if anxiety is excessive and affects your daily life, it may be time to see a mental health professional.

At age twenty-nine, John was always terrified of doing something—anything—wrong. He thought people would judge him harshly if he made a mistake, just as his father had done during his childhood and youth. When his girlfriend invited him to meet her family, a highly educated group of people, he was quite worried that he might say or do something silly. The week leading up to the visit, he felt tense and jittery. During dinner, he found it impossible to project his natural self. His stress led him to stutter, which generated even more tension; so much that he eventually left early, embarrassed and full of anger and shame, claiming he had a sudden headache.

John had experienced what is known as a self-fulfilling prophecy, in which he ended up bringing on his worst nightmares because of his dismay and unnecessary concern about messing up.

One of the best ways to learn is through our mistakes: they provide valuable feedback and highlight areas to work on and improve.

Moreover, most people prefer imperfect people—especially those who are comfortable with their imperfections. Imperfections, after all, are what make us human and attractive. Sharing our flaws creates intimacy and fosters close relationships. For that reason, it may be better for our mental health to laugh at our blunders, rather than hiding or fearing them.

Accepting our defects and being open about them frees us from the pressure of being "exposed."

After all, . . . what's the worst that can happen?

15.Practice assertiveness

To be passive is to let others decide for you. To be aggressive is to decide for others. To be assertive is to decide for yourself. And to trust that there is enough, that you are enough.

-Edith Eva Eger

The Dorland Medical Dictionary [7], an old companion during my years at medical school, defines assertiveness as a pattern of behavior characterized by a confident statement or affirmation without need for approval. This is to assert the person's point of view without aggressively threatening that of another (assuming a position of dominance) or allowing another person to ignore or deny our position (resign to a position of submission).
Assertive communication is intended to respect the limits of oneself and others. It also implies an interest in meeting needs and desires through cooperation.

Tony, 39, feared his family's annual Christmas dinner. Every December 24, the same scene unfolded:

Tony was irritated by his family's disregard and dismissive attitudes but repressed any response until he exploded with rage. His sister, Rita, 30, took the opposite approach: She agreed with everyone, fearing to express what she thought so she didn't hurt anyone. Both, however, felt tense, clumsy, resentful, and unappreciated. Tony seemed immature in the eyes of his family. Rita gave the impression of distance and infantility. They both felt their family was a "pending issue" that they couldn't manage.

Tony, Rita, and others like them would do well to remember some key points: We need to express ourselves without waiting too long. We have to expose our position without letting tension grow and without apologizing for saying what we think or feel. We should speak calmly, respectfully, and directly. When people know that we're giving them our honest opinion rather than adopting a submissive position, they're more likely to treat us with respect. By being assertive, yet not aggressive, people are more likely to listen to us. And if they don't, it's not our problem anymore.

The style we adopt when dealing with others is crucial. It determines who loves us, hates us, seeks us, or avoids us, more than our beliefs, ideas, or opinions.

According to the book *Cognitive Behavioral Therapy* (2008) [8], "Assertive communication of personal opinions, needs and limits has been conceptualized as the middle term of behavior, which lies between passive and aggressive ineffective responses." Such communication "emphasizes expressing feelings directly, but in a way that does not become aggressive."

If the actions of others threaten one's boundaries, one communicates it to avoid escalation. **In contrast, aggressive communication serves to judge, personalize, threaten, lie, break down confidence, and infringe on limits.**

At the opposite side of the spectrum of dialectics there is passive communication. Victims can passively allow others to violate their limits. Later, they can even make things worse by counterattacking with a desire of revenge or passive-aggressive behaviour.

Assertive communication seeks to transcend these extremes by appealing to the shared interest of all parties; **it focuses on the subject, not the person.** Aggressive and/or passive communication, on the other hand, can mark the end of a relationship, and reduce self-esteem.

In short, assertiveness involves saying what we think without hiding anything and not by saying the first thing that comes to our mind, following an impulse.

Assertive people tend to have the following characteristics:

– They feel free to express their feelings, thoughts, and desires.

– They can initiate and maintain healthy relationships with other people.

– They know their rights and expect them to be respected.

– They have control over their anger. This does not mean that they suppress this feeling; it means they control anger and talk about it in a reasoned way.

– They are willing to compromise with others, instead of always wanting to be right.

– They tend to have good self-esteem.

– They take into account both their needs and those of others.

Here are some ideas to start training in assertiveness.

1. Start off slowly. Facing strong arguments without being prepared predicts failure. Try to be assertive in slightly tense situations such as, for example, requesting to be seated in a different place in a restaurant. Then progress gradually until you can face more challenging circumstances, such as talking to our spouse about a marital situation or with our boss about a pay raise.

2. Learn to say no. People are concerned about the idea that saying no to others is selfish. It's not. In fact, setting healthy boundaries is essential for having healthy relationships.

3. Put guilt aside. Being assertive can be difficult, especially if you've always adopted a passive or a "crowd-pleaser" approach most of your life. The first few times, you may feel awkward. But we must remember that being assertive is vital to our well-being. **The outspoken behavior that involves self-advocacy in a way that respects others is not wrong**; it is a healthy attitude.

Sometimes, we may unintentionally perpetuate our feelings of guilt with negative thoughts, such as "I'm a bad person, because I felt unable to lend money to my friend." Instead, we can counter with a positive affirmation like "I deserve financial stability and not to put myself in jeopardy."

4. Explain your needs and feelings. Please don't assume that someone will automatically know what we need. Sometimes it has to be said directly. Again: you have to be specific, transparent, honest, and respectful.

When we discuss with our partner, for example, we might be tempted to say something like, "You have no idea what my life is like, and you're a selfish jerk." Instead, we might say, "I'm exhausted, and I'd like to get more help with the kids." What also helps is to moderate our anger and speak about the way we feel, like "I feel very lonely, and I would appreciate you spending more time with me."

No one can be offended if, during a discussion or negotiation, we express how we feel rather

than resort to personal disqualifications. And if offense is taken, it's most likely their problem.

It is essential to keep this in mind: we are transmitting to the other person what happens to us, and she will determine what behavior she chooses based on it. The ball is in their court.

Try to focus on the real problem, not trivialities. In other words, are you outraged because you had to get out of bed five times the night before because the baby was crying? Be clear and specific about your needs: "I'm upset that I went to check on the baby five times last night, and I need you to get up at least twice a night to help me."

Forget about previous offenses, and avoid getting personal.
5. Avoid unnecessary expressions like "you never" or "you always." Refer exclusively to what you are concerned about at that precise moment. Refrain from bringing up situations from the past, especially if they have already been addressed.

16. Live your life on your our own terms

Being wise selfish means taking a broader view and recognizing that our own long-term individual interest lies in the welfare of everyone. Being wise selfish means being compassionate.
- Dalai Lama

Ricardo is a renowned vascular surgeon going through a midlife crisis. He once said to me, *"Right now, I feel angry with myself: I think all my life I've lived trying to impress a lot of people who don't care about me and who I don't even really like ..."*
Bronnie Ware's book, The Top Five Regrets of the Dying: A Life Transformed by the Dearly Departing (10), is based on her years of experience working as a nurse. She describes and analyzes the regrets of terminally ill patients who have accepted the end is imminent and look back at their lives.
The most important conclusion is that in general, people regret having worked too hard and expressed their feelings very little. They wish they'd made other choices. They regret losing touch with close friends and putting others' expectations above their own values.

Ware recounts countless confessions and feelings expressed by patients over many years. She grouped them into several main categories, all which demonstrated a common trend: stay authentic to what matters most; stay true to yourself.

So, what can we do to make sure we live a life that has meaning? How can we discover our true selves? What strategies can we use to identify and challenge external and internal obstacles that prevent us from pursuing not only our dreams but also our core values?

Here are some essential steps:

1. Take time to find out what you really want.

During our early years, we count on our family to convey out signs (smiles, rewards, frowns, scolding, etc.) to indicate whether we are doing something right or wrong. As we grow up, if we have learnt who we are, our values, and what we want to reflect on our lives, there is less reason to seek the validation of others.

For most of us, knowing who we are and where to go is a challenge.

According to research by the Federal Center for Disease Control, about 40 percent of Americans have not determined a sense of purpose in their lives. It's easy to say, "live your life on your own terms," but if we haven't discovered those terms, we can feel like we are drifting through our own existence. When we are unsure of what we want, we go through life without a clear direction. Deciphering our principles can help us maintain a course no matter what life throws in our way. Maybe it's good to start by asking ourselves: What is it that genuinely motivates us? What do we really care about? Our family, our community, and society in general will have a lot to say about what we should be doing. Still, ultimately, only we can answer these questions. We're, after all, in control.

Thinking about what we want is not a selfish attitude, but a fundamental part of the process of getting to know ourselves. Exploring about our desires in life does not mean leaving others aside; it often means the opposite. Deciding what is essential to us involves recognizing the people who are important to us. It means determining that they are a priority in our lives and that caring for them is part of what makes us happy.

When we live a life with purpose, everything around us has more meaning. We are likely to be kinder, more considerate, and more understanding of each other regardless of the circumstances in life. When we are satisfied with our lives, we can display the best version of ourselves.

 If we like to socialize with certain friends or groups of people, do we make it a priority? If we love a particular activity, how much time do we invest in it?

So, let's ask ourselves what motivates us, what is it that we do effortlessly and enjoy. These pleasures that make us feel that time flies by and everything flows naturally when we are doing them; something we would actually pay to do.We all have something to discover that ignites our souls; something we are passionate about.

And if we're not sure what we're excited about, maybe it's time to try different things until we discover what it is.

It is also crucial not to assume that we know ourselves too well and typecast ourselves. Sometimes, it's hard to realize what you want, but the idea is to explore, keep moving, and not take anything for granted. I discovered this from personal experience. Years ago, I didn't think that I had the patience to write a book, and I didn't think this was something I enjoyed. One day, I decided to write a series of articles with the idea of making a summary of concepts that I would have liked to have had at the beginning of my medical training as a psychiatrist. I came to realize that I could not have been more wrong at the time, and I have already managed to publish three books with many other possibilities in mind. I love writing, and it has become a very satisfying part of my life—something that helps me to make sense of the world and something that makes me jump out of bed in the morning.

2. Set specific goals.

Many times, people tend to set too imprecise, non-specific goals, such as, "I want to be happy," which is commonplace. It is essential to set out concrete objectives that will lead to a tangible result.

Another mistake we make is to adopt a negative approach to our aims. Instead of, "I want to look my best, so I'm going to eat healthily," we say, "I'm too overweight. I must lose weight now."

A better strategy would be to list the actions that are in line with what we are looking for, and then to think in specific actions that can be undertaken to approach these aspirations.

We should set up SMART goals, which means specific, measurable, achievable, results-focused, time-limited goals. Develop a personalized action plan to achieve these objectives with clear steps, within a reasonable time.

3. Ignore our internal critic.

Sometimes, it is not easy to move out of our comfort zone; we often feel an internal voice that warns us of the risks and potential conflicts. It is a voice inspired perhaps by ideas received during childhood that seek to keep us safe although at the expense of sometimes not following our instincts.

If we really want to change something in our lives, we must adopt a zero-tolerance policy toward our inner critic. When we feel that this repressive mechanism begins to activate, it is best to suppress it without questioning it, just by opposing an alternative idea.

Let's say, for example, we want to change an unfair situation in the workplace. Our inner voice warns us against this as we could receive a bad reputation. The opposite thought would be about the benefits that we can gain by being more assertive by expressing our point of view.

4. Put aside the expectations of others
Well, this is the tough part. We must try to stop worrying about what others might think of us. This can be very difficult, especially if our lives have been dominated by the opinions of our parents, teachers, or friends. However, doing so is a necessary and healthy step actually to march to the beat of your own drum. **Always trying to please others can be an unbearable task and the most direct path to dissatisfaction and unhappiness.**
Constantly worrying about what other people say immobilizes us. Simply put, we cannot take adequate steps in our lives when our actions are always determined by others.
We tend to think that the more we contribute to make others happy, the more they will give back to us. With this philosophy, there is a risk of attracting people into our lives who are more than happy to keep on taking from us. After years of this repeated behavior, we will end up exhausted, resentful, and with feelings of emptiness.

Maybe we should start asking ourselves the right questions to get the answers we need: Who said we need to have children to have a fulfilling life? Is it absolutely essential to go to university to be someone in life? Do we have to support the political or religious beliefs passed on from our family? Is it beneficial to be submissive and discreet to make progress in life? The list can be endless.

It is important to trust our instincts. If we know what our core values are, we can rely on our own decision-making skills as long as they are in alignment with them.

It is essential to not rely on external validation. **If we're going to make mistakes, let them be OUR mistakes.**

Setting limits for others and being true to ourselves requires courage, but failing to do so will inevitably lead to a feeling of stagnation that can spiral to anxiety or depression.

In a well-documented scientific experiment, a group of monkeys was placed in a cage. They had enough food and water inside their habitat to survive. There was a bunch of bananas of the best quality at the top of the cage, and they could only be reached by climbing a ladder that had been placed there for that purpose. After a while, a jet of iced water was sprayed whenever the monkeys wanted to reach the bananas. They all received the same treatment. The sprinkler system was activated automatically every time one of the primates climbed the ladder to reach the bananas. This continued for a few days. Soon after, every time a monkey prepared to climb the ladder to take a banana, the other monkeys stopped it by shoving and hitting. Knowing the outcome that awaited them when they tried to take the bananas, none of the monkeys dared to climb the ladder.

After a while, a variant was introduced to the experiment: A new subject who knew nothing about the issue of bananas and water jets was added to the group. After seeing the bananas hanging over his head, the newly introduced monkey set out to climb the ladder, although a rain of blows from the other monkeys prevented it. A few days later, they replaced another monkey with a new one. The same thing happened with every new subject that entered the cage. Therefore, they replaced all the original monkeys and this remaining group prevented any newcomers from reaching the bananas. After a few weeks in the cage, none of the original monkeys were left.

Although none of these monkeys had ever received a jet of iced water in retaliation for trying to take a banana, they didn't even attempt to do it.

17. Share the pain

Shared joy is a double joy; shared sorrow is half sorrow.

– Christoph August Tiedge

In this era of rampant narcissism, many people are more willing to raise their voices to talk about themselves rather than to listen. But there are also others—the shy, the more insecure, those who think they are bothersome and that their concerns are trivial—who tend to keep everything to themselves. It is not uncommon for family members to hide their pain from each other. The greater the suffering, the greater the tendency toward self-isolation. Those who are suffering have learned to do it this way. They get used to enduring pain in private, to keeping it inside, and to moving on with their lives. Even during therapy, they are reluctant to disclose everything so as not to bother their therapist!

Needless to say, **this denial of our needs can be damaging for our psyche, making our spiritual burdens more cumbersome than they should be.**

A team of neurologists from the Laboratory of Social and Affective Neuroscience at the University of Haifa in Israel conducted an experiment (11) with 20 volunteer couples to determine what happens in the brain when one partner experiences pain and the other holds their hand. It was the first time the experiment had been conducted while scanning both individual's brain waves simultaneously.

The experiment showed that brain waves in the α-μ frequency are synchronized between couples when they hold hands during an induced pain situation. These waves are associated with the perception of pain and empathy. The rest of the brain waves did not record significant changes.

The important observation here is that this synchronization can reduce pain. The Israeli team's hypothesis is that physical contact generates empathy and, in turn, generates endorphins that reduce the perception of pain to some degree. Research still has a long way to go in this area.
In the meantime, what does seem certain is that sharing the pain helps us to cope with it.

The fact that mood changes occur simply by talking to someone and by feeling heard is remarkable. Sharing our concerns can bring great relief. We know that expressing our feelings during times of loss and distressing circumstances that accompany our lives helps to alleviate suffering and heals the wounds of the soul.

At this point, we must differentiate between sharing pain with neurotically and constantly complaining. We are not talking about people who only want to project negativity on us without resolving anything or looking for solutions: In the long-term grievance, opposite to what complainers think, weakens them. A complaining approach implies an attitude of dependence and victimization. If frequently practiced and not fixed, it can become chronic. In reality, constant complaints cover up self-devaluation and denial of one's own ability to work problems out. The chronic complainers request, subtly and manipulatively, third-party support often based on pity.

Sharing pain sincerely and without complaint, on the other hand, means taking responsibility for our lives and asserting ourselves by overcoming problems. To express sorrow is to bring out the vulnerability and consequent greatness that our humanity entails. The honest, open-hearted relief of emotions should not be confused with being demanding; our troubled feelings of confusion and sorrow ask only for attention and to be listened to. The better we become at verbalizing our pain, the more we are able to suppress the roots of our suffering. As negative feelings are shared, we achieve perspective and our thoughts are more easily organized in our heads. We then adopt the position of the spectator of our own difficulties with the necessary detachment and calm.

18. Compare yourself wisely

I did this to myself back then, compared my accomplishments at twenty-three to those of spectacularly successful people (Picasso at twenty-three was finishing his Blue Period; Mick Jagger was writing "19th Nervous Breakdown"; Joan of Arc had rescued France, been burned at the stake, and been dead for four years).
— **Tom Barbash, *The Dakota Winters***

Comparison with myself brings improvement; comparison with others brings discontent.
— **Betty Jamie Chung**

Comparisons are unpleasant and unproductive. The game of comparisons is as old as humanity.

Studies show that time on social media increases the chance of depression linked to fruitless comparisons and has a negative impact on well-being. Presumably, all these glamorous posts, which can be linked to rampant narcissism in our society, only serve to reinforce unrealistic standards.

Some people have a tendency to perceive some circumstances in a way that makes them feel bad about themselves or their lives. It is generally situations in which someone makes them believe they lack something in their life that others have (something they probably hadn't even thought about until it was pointed out).

A patient of mine once told me:

"Reading posts about everyone's vacation kills me. Having three children, I could never afford things like that. Furthermore, these constant Facebook notifications never stop."

Let us then explore how to avoid wasting our own satisfaction by falling into the comparison trap.

Here are some suggestions:

1. Make yourself aware and avoid sterile comparisons.

Start to acknowledge situations that trigger the inclination to compare ourselves to others.

Social media is here to stay and it is considered important for most of us. As we mentioned before, they are often a source of comparisons. What about in other situations? Is there anyone who continually brags about their life, or asks you questions about yours that are intended to make you feel inferior? Do certain activities, such as walking around a luxury mall or driving around an expensive neighborhood, make you feel unhappy with your life or somehow make you feel inferior when everything was okay just an hour before? Make a list of whom and what you compare to frequently. Write down how it affects you negatively and why it is really time wasted. Make a conscious effort to restrain yourself next time: for every judgment that generates discouragement, propose another one that provides you self-satisfaction. Indeed, we can always compare ourselves to someone who appears to be worse off than us. **This does not mean being glad that they are in a worse position, nor is it conformism, but it is putting things into perspective.**

2. Remember that other people's "exteriors" cannot be compared to what's happening in the inside.
Even if we are really close friends with someone, we can't judge their circumstances based on what they show. Remember that people carefully choose which version of their life to exhibit on social media and they do the same with the lives they live publicly. It is not unusual, for example, to be surprised when a couple who appeared to be happy and robust on social media announce their divorce.
Of course, we should always wish the best for others, but if the perception of others people's lives gives you reason to feel bad about yours, remember that you don't really know what's going on behind closed doors. The reality may be quite different from what's revealed.

3. Repeat whenever necessary: Money or luxury do not buy happiness, and they never will.
It is well established, as we mentioned in another section, that wealth, beyond what provides some

security in life, is not linked to an increase in happiness or well-being. The purchase of material possessions provides a temporary feeling of joy that, in a short time, fades away; its inevitable inability to supply lasting happiness can lead to disappointment.

4. Be grateful for simple pleasures in your life and try to resist any urge to think that it is not enough.
If we commit ourselves to be deeply grateful for all the good things in our lives and remind ourselves of it every day, we will be much less exposed to comparison and jealousy. If someone or something triggers that unpleasant emotion of negative correlation, stop and consider what's good in your life right now. There will be plenty of examples.

5. Utilize comparison as motivation to improve what actually matters to you.
The very human inclination to desire what others have is futile unless, of course, what we see and covet in another person is something positive and admirable, such as their generosity, kindness, or other qualities.
Who do you admire? What types of comparisons might be healthy for you? Who inspires you to live a better, purposeful life?
Imagine if we could elevate the game of comparison to a useful art form. Let us stop being enslaved by its darkest part, which only develops feelings of sadness and emphasizes the lack of something in our lives. Instead, let's use analogy in an intelligent way to make

a better person out of ourselves and maybe even make our little niche in the world a better place.

6. Compare with yourself.
Sometimes we can assess our current situation by relating it to our past.
This reframing technique is widely used by psychotherapists around the world. It helps the patient acknowledge the progress they have made from the beginning of therapy.
It's a useful strategy,used when people are discouraged by what they consider to be a stalemate in their healing process. When they are able to see the improvement they have made from the beginning, however small it may be, there is a sense of well-being.
So, instead of completely resisting any kind of comparison with others, why not just redirect it to the past and present self and compare ourselves with ourselves?
We're constantly evolving. Who we are today is the result of the decisions we made yesterday. We are in a state of constant change. We make decision after decision, and the direction will always be toward expansion, as it is part of human nature.
So, if we find ourselves that we are comparing to others, let's stop for a moment and redirect our thoughts. Instead of succumbing to the temptation of comparing ourselves to someone else, let's ask a few questions:

What are you doing today that you couldn't have done a few years ago?

What new choices have you made or what further steps have you taken that have ended in a move toward a new path in your life?

What are your achievements this year compared to last year at this time? How has your life progressed?

In other words, how did you continue to turn into a new and improved version of yourself?

This is what really matters. Matching ourselves to others in an unfruitful way is an inaccurate and unreliable measuring rule, and it is unproductive.

Helena, a young marketing specialist, came to consultation suffering from depression. From the outset, she told me she felt like a failure in both her career and life.

What had happened? It was revealed that she'd been watching a lot of her friends' posts on social media. One of them had just been promoted to a management role and now led a team of people for the first time. Another had posted photos of his first business trip to Asia. Another friend had just signed a mortgage for her first home. Someone else had bought an expensive sports car. Two other friends had announced their engagements, and someone else had got married and posted some impressive pictures.

"I feel like I 'm a loser," she said, shrinking even further into her chair. *"Everyone else is doing amazing things with their lives. I want to be happy for them, really.*

But I get depressed when I realize how far behind I am in comparison to their accomplishments."

When I asked her what she meant by being so "behind" her friends, this was her response: *"I'm 28 years old, and I still don't have an exciting job. I haven't traveled anywhere on business. I don't earn enough to buy a house or even a new car. And now I don't even have time for a boyfriend, when it seems that all my friends are getting engaged or married. I feel terrible."*

"And if that's not bad enough, my high school reunion is taking place next summer. Everyone will display their achievements and boast about their work. Then I'll feel even more depressed."

Over time Helena recognized the positive aspects of her own life: she had received a pay raise, had been given a leadership role in a new project in her department, and has even been recognized and praised by her boss because of her high standards.

She noted down the progress she had made, which would likely provoke recognition from more than one of her colleagues.

She recalled that her mother, who was very focused on appearances, used to compare her with her friends' children, much to Helena's resentment. Now she recognized that she had been doing the same thing to herself.

She went to her reunion and was able to see for herself that appearances on social networks are just that: appearances.

One apparently happy couple had a heated argument in front of everyone. A successful businessman who constantly showed off his achievements on Facebook ended up in a drunken state and was challenging everybody to a fight. The popular girl with the perfectly toned figure turned out to be addicted to cosmetic surgery.

That night Helena learned that she was in control of choosing who to compare herself to, and that her choices had an impact on her well-being.

It's easy if we make the effort not to compare yourself to anybody else, especially when it involves material things. If I'm worried about other people and what they are doing, about all the attention they are getting, I'm not going to be able to do what I'm capable of doing. It's a surefire way to make yourself miserable.

Not only will it divert you from doing the best you can, but people who have too much regard for social judgments find themselves chronically unstable, vulnerable, intimidated, and plain miserable. You can't be jealous and happy at the same time. The happier the person, the less consideration she gives to what others around her are accomplishing.

Comparing yourself to other people is like comparing apples to peaches. They are two separate things. Sadhguru, an Indian mystic, puts it beautifully: "If you look at a mango tree and a coconut tree, and your idea of being better is being tall, then what you will do with the mango tree is you chop off all the branches except

the highest one, hoping that it will grow. It is never going to be a coconut tree – it is only going to be a crippled mango tree. This is what happens to most human beings. **They become crippled because they are trying to be better than someone else.**"
If you're a Mango tree, what's the point of comparing yourself to a coconut tree? If you're a beautiful peacock, what's the point of comparing yourself to an eagle? That's pointless.
If I'm a peacock, I simply want to be the very best peacock I can be. That's all I can do: to come close to my level of competency, not somebody else's. I have nothing to do with theirs, only mine.
Concentrate on displaying the best version of yourself, not a deformed variant of someone else.

Envy, jealousy, and criticism can become cancerous. They hurt the person who feels them rather than the person they're directed toward."
The Buddha supposedly said, "Holding on to anger is like grasping a hot coal with the intent of throwing it at someone else; you are the one who gets burned." And someone else once compared holding a grudge to eating rat poison and thinking the rat will die.
The point is, emotions like envy, jealousy, or anger don't hurt the person they're directed at. They hurt the person who feels them.
Learn to let go of such emotions.

The reason we battle with self-doubt is because we compare our behind-the-scenes with everyone else's highlight reel.

Correlations make you feel superior or inferior, and neither serves a useful purpose.

19. Find meaning in life without becoming obsessed

It did not really matter what we expected from life, but rather what life expected from us. We needed to stop asking about the meaning of life, and instead to think of ourselves as those who were being questioned by life—daily and hourly. Our answer must consist, not in talk and meditation, but in right action and in right conduct. Life ultimately means taking the responsibility to find the right answer to its problems and to fulfill the tasks which it constantly sets for each individual.

— Viktor E. Frankl, *Man's Search for Meaning*

In 1942, psychiatrist Viktor Frankl, his wife, and his parents were deported to the Nazi ghetto of Theresienstadt. His father passed away half a year later due to the deplorable living conditions. The following year, Frankl and his wife were transferred to the infamous Auschwitz death camp, where over a million people would be assassinated. He was then transferred to two other camps, separated from his mother and his wife, who would eventually disappear.

During this period, Frankl came to believe that the only way he could survive and maintain his sanity was to hold to a sense of meaning and purpose. He would later quote philosopher Friedrich Nietzsche, who wrote: "He who has a *why* to live can bear almost any how." For Frankl, the meaning came from serving as a doctor for his fellow inmates. After being released from imprisonment, Frankl dedicated his life to advocating towards the value of seeking meaning in life as a protection against suffering, finding that meaning had guided him through the Holocaust and formed the basis of his philosophy (12).

Countless articles and bibliographic material available on the internet promise to guide us to success, wealth and happiness. But when it comes to actually discovering the meaning of life, the information is scarcer. Why is that?

Perhaps it is because we perceive the meaning of life as a mysterious and secret concept that takes a whole lifetime to discover.

Philosophers and monks spend decades studying ancient texts and meditating, trying to understand the purpose of life, why did the universe granted us life, and what we are supposed to do with it.

But what dilemma troubles us most when it comes to seeking the meaning of life? That nothing we do matters, and therefore we don't matter at all?

We have to figure out this meaning. It provides us with an anchor, a ground wire; it allows us to look back and say, "Everything I do has a purpose."

Without this meaning, it can be easy to get lost in a daily struggle. More than anything else, we *need* a purpose in life.

Those who find their lives make sense are generally happier, friendlier, and healthier people, both mentally and physically.

But that's the million-dollar question: how do we turn our lives into something significant?

Maybe it's a lot simpler than it appears. Perhaps we don't need to take a gap year to join Buddhist monks somewhere remote in Asia.

The secret of a meaningful life could be to remind ourselves every day to do the right thing, love to the fullest, pursue fascinating experiences and perform tasks that bring illumination to our world—not to do these things only because we are trying to find meaning in life, but because these activities are rewarding and good for our well-being.

It is not a question of discovering ancient secrets and hidden truths inaccessible to the general public, nor is it about giving up all the material desires and needs in your life.

It's about waking up to yourself and realizing that the answers you're looking for are probably already there inside you, just waiting to be discovered.

Maybe the key to finding that meaning is to stop searching, take a break, and just enjoy.

There is no need for sudden changes in our lives, such as getting rid of all our assets or giving up our jobs; these things are not that viable in the modern world. Instead, a positive step would be to take a moment to recognize our life and everything we've experienced.

What does this mean?

It signifies that we must take time to appreciate the everyday situations we go through and extract meaning from these experiences—things like chatting with friends, establishing ties with neighbors, helping in our community, finding personal satisfaction in our work (and if we can't, just looking for a more suitable job). This is what increases our social connections, and the more significant these are, the less likely we will feel lost and inclined to think our lives are meaningless. We are able to find simple comforts among these little rituals that we do for ourselves because they provide a sense of normality to our lives.

These daily habits and rituals serve to keep our lives focused and balanced. Let's find something to wake up for and set goals to follow every day. **Let's make the unappealable decision to be happy every single day of our lives, regardless of the circumstances.**

And most importantly, let's stop overthinking.

There is no evidence that obsessively searching for meaning in our lives leads to finding it. The harder we look for it, the more it slips away.

While a meaningful life is associated with greater happiness, the obsessive pursuit of it can result in the opposite outcome.

The meaning of life is not something we have to think about; it is something that we continuously create ourselves.

And that makes sense. It's the same with love. We don't have to convince ourselves that we love our partner, our family, and friends. We just do.

Maybe life is not meant to be comprehensively understood, but simply lived.

Maybe we don't need to know how to make our lives meaningful. We just need to know that they already are.

20. Adapt to change

It is not the strongest of the species that survives, nor the most intelligent. It is the one that is most adaptable to change.

- Charles Darwin

Life events are constantly changing. Loved ones pass away; relationships end, work ventures are concluded. People advance in their professional career, some may be fired (which can sometimes mean progress ...), couples join in matrimony or separate (another advance, sometimes...), babies are born, our elders pass away.

When confronted with change, why is it some people find motivation and opportunity, while others find only hopelessness and pain? This refers to all kinds of changes because, contrary to what many believe, positive changes can be as tricky to assume as negative changes.

Those working in psychosociology have been researching on adaptability to change for a long time.

In 1983, the U.S. Department of Justice ruled that the giant monopoly on Bell System communications would be divided into several smaller companies—a situation that would impact on the lives of thousands of people. Psychologist Salvatore Maddi saw an opportunity to analyze how people react to change in their lives.

For the next 12 years (13), Maddi and his team at the University of Chicago used the telephone company's Illinois Bell division as their lab. They followed the reaction of hundreds of employees and monitored everything conceivable. Researchers took notes and asked questions—as the workers moved from one office to another, as the national economy progressed and worsened again, as children were born, as marriages ended and mortgages were paid, as governments changed.

Six years after the beginning of the investigation, about half of the people in the follow-up group were laid-off, while the other half remained at the company. Maddi and his team continued to monitor both groups for the next six years. What they found was captivating. Most people, regardless of whether they kept their jobs or lost them, suffered unfortunate consequences. There were divorces, strokes, cancers, suicides, heart attacks, alcoholism, amongst other addictions. The offices of "Ma Bell," as the company was known among people, became disaster areas filled with the remnants of its workforce.

But a third of those in both groups not only survived but prospered and thrived. They did not suffer heart attacks or marital problems, nor did they fall into any patterns of addiction. Of these individuals, those who stayed at Illinois Bell became high-ranking leaders in the new organization. Those who were fired became pioneers of their new companies.

The most surprising finding was how "normal" people in the adaptive third were. On paper, they looked like everyone else. It's not necessarily that they adapted more easily because they experienced fewer stressful experiences. Neither was it because they had better bosses. Not because they had happier lives at home. They weren't more polite. They weren't smarter. They didn't have more sophisticated titles or more manageable jobs. They didn't have a privileged childhood and they weren't born with any unique genetic gifts.

What separated the "adaptive group" from everyone else was surprisingly uncomplicated: while everyone else dwelled on their fate and staggered along, continuously searching for answers, they just stood up, dusted themselves off, and kept going. They exhibited what Maddi describes as "existential courage."

While many Illinois Bell employees looked around and found nothing but a thick, confusing fog in all directions, they did what most of us do instinctively when we get lost. They backtracked their steps. They obsessively looked for a reason as to why this tragedy was happening to them. They longed for the good old days. When investigators asked employees about their plans for the future, they responded anxiously. When they finally sketched out an answer, their perception of the future looked strangely similar to that of the past.

They wanted to "go back" to a place that no longer existed.

The people in the "adaptive third" had a different outlook. They also wondered what change meant. But instead of trying to find an explanation for it by asking the universe what they had done to deserve this experience, they decided to make sense of doing what they could to fix the problem now that it had happened.

This could be the most significant lesson in adaptation. **Instead of asking why good people have bad things happen to them, adaptive people turn the equation around and wonder what good people can do when bad things happen.**

When the shadow of change descends on people, human brains sometimes wonder: What does this mean? Why me? Our minds then launch a large-scale search for answers to resolve our confusion. But we don't all look at the same place.

Roxane Cohen Silver [14], of the University of California-Irvine, found that two out of three widows, parents who have lost a child, victims of terrorism, child abuse, and natural disasters will intrinsically seek meaning from the past. They will try to find some explanation for their suffering. For decades, psychologists assumed that this was a universal reaction after a traumatic change and, therefore, the path to healing required to finding an explanation.

But maybe they were wrong.

In relation to many studies carried out over the past three decades, Silver found that one in three victims of psychological trauma tend look no further than to reasons as to why they are suffering. It is this third portion that turns out to be the most well-adjusted, weeks, months, and years later.

What then?

When change arrives, it is helpful to accept it as gracefully as possible. We may not believe that we deserve it, or we may simply not be ready for it, but the only way forward in terms of progress is to embrace adversity with positivity.

The area where the most considerable changes are occurring is in the employment sector.

Laws are changing at the pace of globalization, and salary earners do not always feel protected, with cases of adverse work relationships becoming more common, as well as harassment.

Some organizations and companies seek productivity at any cost, awarding promotions to those with personality disorder traits, who often compensate for their inability to lead and their ineptitude by a lack of scruples. This generally results in the opposite of the desired: This can lead to increased cases of bullying in the workplace, an unhealthy working environment, and absenteeism or employee turnover increases. Consequently, some people can become engaged in long and exhausting workplace disputes. They maintain a flawed working relationship that only serves to harm them and their own mental health, since many employers, knowing that they have a certain power that they use in a harmful way, have time and resources in their favor.

If this relationship continues to worsen, maybe it's a sign that we should look for more favorable conditions elsewhere. Even if the situation is unjust (and that's what trade unions and labor lawyers are for), if we can't change the situation as a whole, maybe it's better to focus on what we can actually improve.

After all, maybe removing ourselves from a toxic working environment could be the best thing that can happen to us. If we want to change the world, as many movements and organizations do, with very praiseworthy ideals, we can try. when doing so, it's important that we remain mindful of our own inner peace and joy, bearing in mind strategies that do work, and following a rational plan: It is ok to be right about something and fight for an ideal, but still, we need to pay our bills by the end of the month.

Let's keep in mind that the universe is not perfect, and never will be, and it would be very dull if it were.

Negative feelings also occur in the event of a dismissal. The first feeling we may experience when we are laid-off is, "How is it possible that they don't need me, after all I've given them?" This is what psychologists call "the narcissistic wound," which sometimes takes the longest to heal.

Occasionally (most times, probably), dismissal is just the result of the dips in the economy and may not be related to our performance (although sometimes employers look for excuses to justify their actions...).

It's not helpful for anyone to take a dismissal personally. In such a circumstance, we would only be adding feelings of anger to our uncertainty and confusion. This would then hinder our recovery period. Some people can't comprehend that being fired doesn't necessarily mean that they did things wrong. Maybe the explanation is much more straightforward: that our boss is an exploiter or that it was a power trip, that he did it just because he could or because he wanted to save money or to plug in someone else ...

The professional world is not always a fair one, and sometimes **it's better to be happy than to be right**, this doesn't imply that we should abandon any kind of formal claim or process if we think we have been treated unfairly—rather, that we should not lose sight of the fact that our tranquility and mental health should be put first.

When a negative change looms, and there are objective and unambiguous signals to indicate this, it's wise to look for alternatives before the change actually happens, if at all possible. For example, if we know that our company is in financial trouble and we start to hear rumors that make everybody feel insecure, why wait until we are fired succumbing to feelings of helplessness and expecting the worst; instead, we should start actively looking for another job there and then. Or maybe it's time to launch ourselves into another career as a freelancer. The idea is to take care of our own priorities rather than worry or to feel upset and helpless.

Emotional changes can be the hardest to accept. For example, in cases of relationship breakups, acceptance is not often a natural choice. You may not feel in the position to have the courage or perception to be objective. In situations like this, we need to process our feelings, and this may take some time. If we feel ourselves stagnating during the process and if we want to address and treat any other related problems at the same time (the propensity to choose the "wrong" type of partner, for example), it may be advisable to consult a therapist.

In short: It's vital that we take responsibility for how we deal with changes. As Dr. Albert Ellis said: "*The best years of your life are the ones in which you decide your problems are your own. You do not blame them on your mother, the ecology, or the president. You realize that you control your own destiny.*"

If transitions in our lives seem overwhelming, we don't have to deal with them on our own. Friends, family, support groups, and therapists are available, but we have to fully acknowledge the situation first and then ask for help, which can be the most difficult step. Sharing any difficulties with our loved ones can make our lives easier. Here, the Buddhist saying, **Pain is inevitable, suffering is optional**, becomes very relevant.

Although we are generally upset by such changes, and having to leave our comfort zone isn't easy, there's no easy way around it. There is no law to dictate that we have to like what happens, but it's our own responsibility to find a way to cope, because change happens, whether we like it or not.

Life can be very hard to sail through in our fast-paced culture. Circumstances are evolving so rapidly these days that by the time we open the box for our new mobile, it's probably already outdated. Learning (at our own pace) to deal with the changes that occur around us is an excellent survival tool. It's about finding a way to "flow" in the most comfortable way possible as we learn to deal with the difficulties that life poses.

Adapting to change is critical; the only thing we have to avoid is immobility. To keep on moving at any pace is crucial. Just moving in one direction, whatever that direction might be, is a vital part of the recovery process when we've been severely affected by a change.

21.Relativize

The greatest wisdom, in my view, is to relativize everything, not to dramatize anything.
-José Saramago

From that point of view, I realized that my hole was not miles deep after all. My father, in fact, could stand on the bottom and it only reached up to his chest. Darkness, you know, is relative.
— **Jodi Picoult, *My Sister's Keeper***

Sometimes life can be overwhelming. Whether events are extraordinary or usual, this feeling can be draining, so it is important to develop strategies to put things into perspective, no matter what happens. Our goal should be to relativize the situation so that it becomes more absorbable and does not crush us under its weight. In exact terms, and using the same analogy, **it is not about the weight, but how we carry it.**
Some people will already be familiar with the value of relativizing. They tend to not refer to anything as terrible or unbearable because they believe that there will always be something worse. Furthermore, they realize that the more negative approach will not solve the problem. Other, emotionally vulnerable people

tend to evaluate circumstances in life as terrible and consequently suffer more.

What helps is learning to assess the true extent of the problem and, above all, to internalize the notion that nothing is as awful or dramatic as we think or as we are led to believe.

Learning to relativize has always been one of the keys to a more serene life. It helps us to improve our interpersonal skills, to better analyze our strengths and weaknesses and, ultimately, to move towards a progressive and continuous evolution.

As is often the case, the theory is not necessarily easy to apply in practice. Who doesn't get stressed before an important job interview or exam? Who has never reacted impulsively to a conflicting situation? Let him who is without sin cast the first stone…

We must ask ourselves about the strategies, the methods, that can be used to limit this type of emotional overflow and to allow ourselves to stop making mountains out of molehills.

Learning to relativize is a priority, a necessity, if we are to live in a harmonious and mentally healthy world. Relativizing also helps us to eliminate certain self-accusatory, destructive, and sterile thinking patterns that oftentimes become a habit.

Our culture, which is immersed in chronic dissatisfaction, often prevents us from realizing the richness of the world around us. It leaves us exposed to any criticism or negative situation to unfold as a true drama with the potential to generate trauma.

We must go beyond these limits, drop the blindfold, and face the truth.

We must learn to question the gravity, extent, and impact of certain external situations in relation to our feelings.

In short, learning to relativize is also learning how to become open and honest with ourselves, and free of external opinions. We must learn how to be kind to ourselves.

How to apply this?

1. Differentiate between subjective perception and objective reality.

When problems arise, regardless of the nature, we often lock ourselves in an ultra-personal reflection which includes suffering, pain, and grief. Self-pity – feeling sorry for ourselves without trying to help ourselves– becomes a foundation of our thinking pattern. However, the cimpact of this on our state of mind can be disastrous, producing a tendency to isolate ourselves and leading us to perceive life from a negative, dark perspective. This is how depression is born.

Learning to relativize implies taking time to breathe, to meditate and to focus on what is really going on.

Maybe a wrong decision has been made; perhaps we are experiencing a problematic or uncomfortable situation; maybe we are suffering an injustice. This does not mean that the situation should prevail over all the surrounding sources of satisfaction available to us.

Sometimes we almost forbid ourselves the right to be happy.

When we adopt this kind of approach, we focus on the core of anguish, eventually surrendering our own powers over to events themselves. We become unable to tell ourselves that better days will come and that the situation we are facing is only transient.

The gap between our own perceptions and objective reality widens.

To relativize, we need to abandon this flow of negative thoughts, beliefs that take over us and affect how we are feeling.

Before sinking into a sea of doubt, **we must ask ourselves the right questions.**

Instead of "Why me?", let's ask ourselves what we can learn from the situation, or what people we admire or respect would do in a similar context. Let's concentrate on our strengths instead of focusing on our vulnerabilities; let's think who we can ask for help...

These are the questions that will help us regain our strength. They will help us to understand that our discouragement is temporary and that the problems we are experiencing can also be part of a learning process and personal development.

It is crucial to look beyond appearances. We need to use our logical reasoning skills, and judge situations based on what's tangible as opposed to focusing on speculation.

Our imagination has a tendency to catastrophize, creating scenarios that never materialize. These ideas

generate anxiety, and questioning them is of outmost importance.
What to do?

1. Distance ourselves emotionally from the problem. When we feel that we can't put things into perspective or that life is too overwhelming, it's time to take a rest and reflect because if our emotions are agitated, we'll probably struggle to reason.
Sometimes we can overreact to a situation. By taking some time to reflect, we can change our focus and obtain new answers.

2. Recognize there are certain things we can't change. It's fruitless and exasperating to worry about something that is out of our control. Accepting that some things can't be changed can bring the relief needed to deal with the situation with a fresh approach.

3. Focus on what we have control over. If we find that we can't change something in its entirety, let's try to identify something, however small, that can be modified. For example, if we lose a job, let's try to identify something that can be done to keep moving: updating a resume, printing brochures to promote a business, posting our services on social media...

4. Try to put ourselves in someone else's shoes. If we are struggling with our own problems and feel desolate, we can always think of the many people who are less fortunate than we are. There are, and many of them. This can bring instantaneous relief.

Adriana is a 36-year-old housewife who came to a consultation suffering from severe depression.

"My life is a heavy burden," she said with discouragement, displaying the body language that reflected her words.

She felt frustrated at work and exhausted by her busy life with her husband and two teenage children. She was looking for something to make her happy but didn't know what.

"It's awful. I don't have to put up with this..." she would say, crying.

Over the months, we tried several therapeutic approaches without significant improvement. One day, I suggested she complete her career as a social worker, which she had abandoned because of ever-present tiredness.

She eventually decided to return to work through an internship.

In the following sessions, she was quieter and more introspective.

Over time, she regained vitality to her life through working in a career she actually enjoyed; she had activated the emotional mechanisms that had been dormant for so long.

What really improved her situation was the fact that she was able to withdraw herself from a reality she had conceived and in return she was able to observe with her own eyes how lucky she was.

"Since working there, I've seen so many people with such diverse problems, so many dramas every day, that I try not to complain about anything anymore. I don't deserve to complain about anything," she told me.

"Nothing else to say, " I replied.

22. Identify and confront irrational beliefs

One should believe only what can be chosen to be true or just. Irrational (or unjustified) beliefs should be avoided because they can have disastrous practical consequences.
     -Mario Bunge

The human brain can create an infinite number of irrational beliefs about how everything should be. These thoughts only serve to hinder our everyday life. When, inevitably, these unrealistic expectations are not met, our neurotic mind evaluates what happens as "unacceptable" while generating self-pitying and frustrating thoughts at the same time. (E.G.: Why is this situation so horrible? This can't be happening to me!)

As we stated in a previous section, we can also "catastrophize" (submerse ourselves in a process psychologists call "cognitive distortion"), not only about things that have happened but also those that could happen... Just thinking about the possibility of something terrible taking place fills us with anxiety.

Psychologist Albert Ellis [15] created a therapeutic method that seeks to discover the irrationalities of our thoughts and thereby heal the painful, dramatized, and exaggerated emotions that result from distorted thought processes. Ellis hypothesis predicts that it is not events that generate emotional states but the way we interpret them. Therefore, if we can change our mental schemas, we should be able to create new emotional states that are less painful and more in line with reality—therefore, more rational and realistic.

Dr. Ellis identified several irrational beliefs; his technique consists of questioning and refuting these beliefs with alternative ideas.

Let's look at some examples:

Irrational Idea No. 1:
"It is an absolute necessity for the human being to be loved and approved by everyone."

Why it's irrational
Trying to please everyone is a direct route to unhappiness; it is an impossible task and demands immense energy. The need to always please will reveal our insecurity and, paradoxically, can result in rejection by others.

Alternative idea
The need for constant approval is not productive or conducive. Not being acknowledged by some can be somewhat frustrating but not catastrophic.

Irrational Idea No. 2:

"To consider yourself valued, you must be very competent, self-sufficient, and able to achieve anything in every area of life."

Why it's irrational

No one is fully competent or capable in any aspect of day to day life. Seeking success is fine; forcing yourself to succeed is frustrating and stressful. Constantly striving for success causes us to compare ourselves to others and to be afraid of failure, which brings internal and external conflicts.

Alternative idea

It's better to focus on the journey rather than the outcome itself. It's more productive to do things in order to feel good than to please others or be better than them.

It is important to pursue our own goals. It is necessary for us to accept our mistakes without criticizing ourselves for them. We need to risk failing from time to time by stepping out of our comfort zone.

Irrational Idea No. 3:

"Some people are 'evil' and malicious and must be held responsible for their actions and punished for their wickedness."

Why it's irrational

Most of the time, people are unaware of the problems they cause or the consequences of their behavior towards others or themselves.

Tolerance towards others and avoiding inflexible postures, generally encourages change.
Alternative idea
Trying to understand someone's actions is better than criticizing or judging. Understanding brings peace and prevents conflict. If there is a calm way to point out to another person their mistakes, this is a much more productive approach. If not, it's okay.
By forgiving others and being less judgmental, we are kinder to ourselves.

Irrational Idea No. 4:
"It's catastrophic and unbearable when things don't go the way we'd like them to go."
Why it's irrational
Whether we like it or not, situations occur that are out of our control.
When things don't go as planned, it's okay to resist and try to change them. But when we can't change them, accepting circumstances as they are is the healthiest and most productive thing to do.
Letting on-going events dishearten us will not help us improve them, and we may make them worse.
Although we can become frustrated about not accomplishing something, the feeling itself is only a consequence of mistakenly considering our desire as a fundamental necessity.
Alternative idea
It is necessary to differentiate between a catastrophic situation and an exaggeration.

Sometimes we paint certain situations with doom and gloom with expressions such as: "It's terrible," "Oh my God, I can't stand it." It would be far more beneficial to replace these statements with more reasonable ones: "This is somehow negative, but not catastrophic," "I think I can tolerate it." We must learn to take tough situations as a challenge from which we can learn.

__Irrational Idea No. 5:__

"Human misfortune has its roots in external conditions and people have little or no ability to control its effects."

Why it's irrational

Although there is a widespread belief that negative emotions cannot be changed and we simply have to suffer them, experience shows that they can be replaced by more productive ones.

It's not about what's happening; it's about how we interpret it.

Alternative idea

When we look objectively at our painful emotions, we need to identify the illogical thoughts and phrases that facilitate them.

If we can radically change our verbalizations, we can transform unconducive and unproductive emotions.

Irrational Idea No. 6:

"If something is or can be dangerous or terrifying, it is necessary to be vigilant, and we have to think about the possibility of this happening constantly."

Why it's irrational

Focusing our attention on something negative in the hope that it won't occur not only doesn't prevent the situation from happening but often only serves to instigate it (remember the idea of "self-fulfilling prophecy"). When it comes to unavoidable situations like illness, personal loss or death, it is not helpful to worry in advance. Worrying about a threatening situation involves exaggerating the possibility it will occur. This anticipation anxiety prevents us from effectively addressing the matter when it actually happens. Most of the dreaded and frightening facts (such as illnesses) tend to be much less catastrophic when they occur. Still, anxiety or fear of events that will undoubtedly occur is even more painful than the feared situation itself.

Alternative idea

Fear doesn't help keep dangers away—quite the opposite.

Most of our concerns are not caused by external dangers but by our distorted internal dialogue.

Irrational Idea No. 7:

"It is easier to avoid than to face certain responsibilities and difficulties in life."

Why it's irrational

The decision-making process of not doing something presumed difficult is usually long and tortuous and, ultimately, more cumbersome than actually taking the plunge. The more we avoid responsibilities the more they will appear. While it's tempting to assume that a comfortable life with no responsibilities would be appealing, experience shows that human happiness is more significant when we are committed to a worthwhile goal.

Alternative idea

A rigid discipline is not necessary. However, it is necessary to plan and establish short- and medium-term goals.

It is necessary to accept that a fulfilling life involves effort. Avoiding problems only serves to make them bigger.

Irrational Idea No. 8:

"You have to always depend on others, and you need someone stronger than yourself to trust in."

Why it's irrational

Complete dependency creates insecurity, which produces low self-esteem, which then generates even more dependency. When we constantly depend on others, we give them control of our well-being. Life starts to feel uncontrollable and unpredictable because others can disappear from our life or pass away.

Alternative idea

It's not terrible to make decisions autonomously. Failure to achieve the goals we set isn't the end of the world, and it does not define us. Nevertheless, it is important to also accept that sometimes we must ask for help, and understand that this does not mean we are failing.

Irrational Idea No. 9:

"Our history determines our current behavior, and things that happened in the past are bound to affect us indefinitely."

Why it's irrational

It is not practicable to use the past as an excuse not to make changes to our present. Solutions applied for past problems do not necessarily work for the issues we face today.

Alternative idea

It is necessary to question those automatic behaviors that we adopted long ago. Our past influences us, it is true, but we can modify the present to obtain different results in the future.

Irrational Idea No 10:

"We must allow ourselves to be affected by the behavior or problems of others."

Why it's irrational

Even if others do things that negatively affect us, our frustration arise from the way we perceive their actions. No matter how angry we feel, they won't necessarily stop doing it.

Getting involved in other people's problems is very often an excuse not to face our own issues and try to rectify them.

Alternative idea

If other people's behaviors upset us, we should let them know in an assertive manner.

We only need to get involved in helping others if they ask us to do so, and only if we feel that we can really do something to help. It is important not to neglect our own problems in the process.

<u>Irrational Idea No. 11:</u>

"There is always an accurate, correct and perfect solution to any problem, and if this ideal solution does not present itself, the result will be a disaster."

Why it's irrational

The search for sanctuary only heightens anxiety. There is no such thing as perfection when it comes to problem-solving.

Perfectionism deals with problem-solving in a much less "perfect" way than if you are a non-perfectionist.

Alternative idea

We shouldn't pretend that we can control every situation or that there are perfect solutions to all problems. We need to accept that life is full of many different shades and not painted in black and white. It is preferable to seek attainable rather than perfect solutions.

There is a deep-rooted drive in many human beings to cling to their learnt and preconceived ideas without verifying their validity as time goes on.
These eleven beliefs presented are oriented to this precisely: to question ideas that do not serve to help us but, in fact, harm or hinder us.
These alternative therapeutic approaches can be compared to training for a long race, where a certain persistent effort is required. We have to design a routine that brings a small challenge every day, in order to break down those ingrained irrational beliefs, to undertake it with increasing intensity and... let time take its course.
In short, this method consists of:
a) Identify every day what irrational beliefs we have held throughout the day. Understand that these are ideas that have caused us emotional discomfort. It is now a good time to write them down on paper.
b) Challenge these fallacious ideas with more fruitful, rational thoughts and insights that will provide us with relief instead of discomfort.
c) Finally, formulate the corresponding rational beliefs.

Example:

- o I'm angry at my neighbor because he didn't say hello to me yesterday. My neighbor should always be polite and greet me.
- o Alternative idea: Is the fact that my neighbor hasn't greeted me really an impediment to my happiness? Is it possible, on the other hand, that he didn't see or acknowledge me because he was worried about his own problems?
- o I would like my neighbor to be more polite. If he is not, it's a shame, but I will respect him anyway, and I will continue to be happy.

It must be emphasized that it is a question of "convincing ourselves" that rational beliefs prevent more damaging circumstances; it's not enough to repeat them automatically like a mantra.

Through this technique of contrasting healthy and productive ideas or beliefs with other more destructive ones, we are able to transform certain negative emotions such as sadness, anguish, anger... into joy, peace, and energy.

23.Get rid of guilt

There's no problem so awful that you can't add some guilt to it and make it even worse.
-Bill Watterson, *The Complete Calvin and Hobbes*

The feeling of guilt stems from betraying our own rules of ethical behavior. If we come from a cultural or family environment that makes us prone to rigorous standards and in which we are judged for not following these precepts, we can be very prone to guilt as a result. The sad reality is that guilt often leads to endless self-blame, which drives us to doubt our potential and all that we could achieve in our lives.

As a psychological phenomenon, guilt can be frustrating and tricky to treat. We become tormented by a tyrant who rumbles within us at the slightest perceived offense; we can feel haunted by those feelings even when we have done nothing to feel guilty for.

Working as a psychiatrist, I have treated many people who feel guilty about thoughts or impulses that, for sure, we all have at some point in our lives and they are not necessarily reprehensible. If we find that someone has deceived us, for example, we might find ourselves fantasizing about revenge (quite violently, in some cases). If our libido is aroused by someone else, it's hard not to have wild fantasies and imagine ourselves ripping off their clothes. And so on.

It is, therefore, essential to determine when feelings of guilt are based on something rational and when they are more or less arbitrary, not connected to reality, and producing unnecessary self-punishment.

Obviously, if we have harmed an innocent person, or if we didn't help someone who was in trouble, knowing that they needed aid and it would have been easy to provide it, it would be considered unethical not to experience remorse. In such cases, if our conscience is not reprimanded, we run the risk of being considered antisocial.

It is crucial, then, to distinguish between rational or "productive" blame as opposed to the kind that is excessively self-critical and mostly unnecessary. Such unfair feelings of guilt have been linked to needless emotional suffering and feelings of self-hatred (sometimes ruthless and relentless enough to drive a person to suicide). If guilt lasts long enough, it can lead to problems associated to anxiety/depression or shame-related conditions such as substance abuse, sexual disorders, and a wide variety of self-sabotage behaviors. So, unless our emotions of guilt are really vital in order to take responsibility for a caused harm or to initiate positive behavioral changes, such feelings are useless.

So, what can be done in the face of this unjustified self-abuse? Because, after all, feelings of guilt tend to culminate in continuous and counterproductive rumination that, in turn, only serve to strengthen our sense of emotional misery.

Guilt is one of those emotions that indicate something important to us, yet, as I said, we have to bear in mind that not all feelings, and indeed not all perceptions of guilt, are rational or have a purpose. The next time we feel guilty we have to be skeptical: is this feeling trying to teach us something useful about our behavior based on our principles, or is it just an emotional and irrational reflection of a situation? The answer to that question will be our first step in helping us to better face blame in the future.

What can unnecessary guilt lead to?

—It can make us hyper-responsible, always striving to lead a life that is "right" (probably in someone else's eyes). It can make us overwork, make too much effort, or be willing to go to extreme lengths to make everyone else happy.

—It can create anxiety, and worry us about every action we take, along with its possible negative consequences for others, even if it means ignoring our needs and desires.

—It can immobilize us, make us feel overwhelmed by the fear of doing, acting, saying, or being "wrong" to the point where we eventually collapse, we give up on ourselves and opt for inactivity and silence, rather than change.

—It can make us deny our own problems because sometimes it is easier to take care of others before ourselves, without realizing that guilt can itself be the motivator of such "generous" behavior.

—It can lead us to ignore the full range of emotions and feelings available to us. Being defeated by guilt or fear of it, we are in danger of closing or blocking ourselves off emotionally and without being able to enjoy the positive experiences of life; our attention will always be focused on the negative.

It would take a whole other book to discuss the guilt sometimes infringed upon us or promoted by certain religions (or, rather, some of their representatives), since they are based on unquestionable dogmas that, if misinterpreted, are impervious to logical reasoning. This can become the perfect tool to support irrational beliefs and promote guilt in its various forms, about matters such as the impureness of premarital sex, the immorality of divorce, or certain sexual tendencies.

How many teenagers suffer chronic guilt about having sexual impulses amid a hormonal storm typical of their age that they cannot (and should not) repress. These feelings of guilt towards these issues are promoted by the rigid moral dogmas of certain members of religious groups who may preach much of divinity but don't realize they are dealing with everyday humane issues? How many gay men and women have been and still are persecuted or victimized because of feeling something that is considered against nature?

Other ideologies can be confronted with evidence and reason, but many people would not dare do this with certain religious beliefs as these are considered to be irrefutable. However, if they are not questioned this can be dangerous and damaging for our mental health. **Let's be clear: having faith in something and developing spirituality through a particular religion are healthy and respectable practices. The opposite is a distorted human interpretation of some of these beliefs along with the benefit that certain religious authorities draw from the guilt they promote.**

To begin this emotional journey toward eliminating unnecessary guilt, I hope to provide some helpful suggestions:

1—Whatever error of judgment prompted us to do something that we might later regret, *Let's always remind ourselves that we did the best we could* and that it was made according to the best criteria at our disposal at that time. Maybe we were simply too angry, anxious, depressed, distracted, or fatigued to be in full possession of our mental faculties. Thus, it can be accepted that, given the particular psychological and physical circumstances in force at the time, no different action could have been taken.

It is imperative to forgive ourselves, and this arises from a compassionate observation of our behavior. It then becomes possible to explore the circumstances surrounding any—alleged—misconduct, without evaluating ourselves in a negative light.

2—Let's consider that, at the time of our wrong doings, we did not have the information we have now. It's unreasonable to blame ourselves for something we would have avoided had we possessed the necessary information.

Let's say we're experiencing feelings of guilt because a good friend asked us to visit them because they were feeling down, and we declined and apologized and refused because we had a prior commitment that was extremely difficult to break. The next day we learn that they are involved in an accident.

On reflection, it seems quite natural to feel guilty for not having been there when the call indicated some amount of distress. As a matter of fact, it might be difficult to dismiss the idea that we could have prevented the accident if we had just stopped by to check on our friend. The temptation to feel somewhat responsible is almost inevitable.

But let us consider whether following such a rigid reasoning process, we are actually being fair to ourselves. In general, blaming ourselves for someone else's misfortune because we could presumably have prevented what was going to happen, from a more objective and humane perspective, is unfair. It is necessary to bear in mind that there are many different situations in which we feel guilt because we consider ourselves overly responsible for the well-being of others.

3—Let's remember that blaming ourselves for a mistake or setback that is out of our control is to assume an intention or volition that may not characterize our behavior at all. If we had possessed the consciousness, intuition, insight, energy, etc. that was required at the time, of course, we would have acted differently. Prolonged regret is, in a way, adding unnecessary pain to the situation.

Do you have a tendency to punish yourself for mistakes that we all make from time to time? If so, as with many of the cases that I'm describing, we need to try not to be so hard on ourselves. We may feel that if we do not blame ourselves, then we will continue to make mistakes, but this is rarely the case. In fact, the more unworried we are about that possibility, the fewer mistakes we generally make.

Let's imagine we damage a car or someone else's during a road accident. We need to ask ourselves: "Realistically, could we have avoided this happening?" The accident was certainly involuntary; otherwise, it wouldn't be classed as an accident. So, let's consider other contingencies that may have contributed to the mishap. It could have been precipitated not only by ourselves but also triggered by other factors. These could include dangerous road conditions, a confusing (and poorly located) traffic signal, the sudden breaking of another driver in the middle of an intersection, a manufacturing defect of our car, etc.

Lots of things can make us feel concerned as why the accident occurred. These might involve us, but they don't indicate that it is necessarily our fault. And even if we take direct responsibility for an accident, are we the only ones that will have gone through this? We all experience having made errors in judgment; when it happens, it's just a matter of asking ourselves: (a) is there anything we can do or learn so that this doesn't happen again, and (b) what's behind this reluctance to forgive ourselves?

4—Let's question whether the standards of behavior we have established for ourselves may be too high. Perhaps our family or religion has encouraged or even compelled us to adopt extremely rigorous standards. We may sometimes feel guilty about not achieving certain goals that we are simply not made for or that go beyond our capabilities.

We all have our limitations, and if we process the message that we are failures because we don't try hard enough, then we are emotionally punishing ourselves. Every time we strongly criticize ourselves for failing at something, we (falsely) should or could have accomplished, we are only adding insult to injury.

We referred earlier to how striving compulsively for perfection is linked directly to failure and low self-esteem. If we don't accept ourselves unconditionally every time we fail to meet expectations that are too high, we will be surrendering ourselves to unhappiness, in the present and future.

5—Let's recognize and respect our right to protect our personal interests. Do we have a hard time saying no because it makes us feel guilty even at the cost of being manipulated? What extremes should we go to meet the needs of others? And here I certainly do not intend to advocate being more inconsiderate or selfish.

On the contrary, generosity and compassionate attitudes are admirable, provided we do not overlook our own needs, in which case those virtues become excuses for not addressing our problems. It is totally justified to value and enforce our needs and beliefs, as much as those of others. If we fail to do so, there is a danger that we will probably end up being treated as human doormats by others who naturally perceive that we should put their needs and desires above our own.

If we continuously put others' interests over our own, we probably should consider the origin of such undervaluing behavior. Do we believe we are not lovable enough, or that we can be accepted only if we serve to please others? Do we satisfy others to the detriment of our own desires? If so, it is essential to challenge these negative assumptions and move forward to overcome any anxieties that prevents us from putting our own needs first.

6—Let's understand the legitimacy of defending our rights. Very tied to the above, this suggestion focuses on feeling good (i.e., not guilty) about our self-affirmation and setting limits comfortably if someone tries to take advantage of us. For example, if we are not interested in a sales call, we don't need to worry about feeling rude if we politely cut the caller short instead of listening patiently to them trying to convince us to buy something. In fact, these calls can be considered inherently disturbing to the extent that they show little or no respect for us. The same applies to human relationships: It is not wrong to set limits (always calmly and politely) when we feel manipulated or imposed on.

Unfortunately, many people will be happy to abuse us if we give them the opportunity. So, it is crucial to remember that there will be numerous occasions when we will need to declare our rights, especially when our instincts tell us that someone wants to take advantage of them.

7—Let's understand that, even if we disagree with others, there is nothing wrong with diligently pursuing our own goals. What should be emphasized here is that, even if we don't want to engage in conflicting or competitive situations, there are times when it is inevitable. So, let's say we tend to blame ourselves every time we are in a position where, in order to succeed, we need to face and defeat someone else. Our self-esteem will hardly be satisfied if our oppressive, dominant, or over-regulatory awareness pushes us to give up.

And finally, and perhaps most importantly:

8—Let's speak compassionately, but firmly, to our inner child, in whom most "programs" of irrational guilt originated. At a younger age, we receive messages from our caregivers that "instructed" us that some of our behaviors were "bad" and should provoke feelings of guilt. At the time, we were not in a position to challenge that idea, we decided that we should be better suited to these rules, punishing ourselves routinely whenever our actions did not meet these indisputable standards.

But now that we are older, we all have the right, based on our own personally structured experience and moral framework, to decide what we believe to be wrong or forbidden as opposed to what is just and permissible; or at least what, in our own value system, is understandable and therefore deserves forgiveness. If, for example, our parents have led us to believe that prioritizing our desires over theirs was selfish, or that becoming "less" than a doctor, lawyer, or engineer was unacceptable; or if a priest categorically proclaimed that premarital sex and masturbation were sinful and would be harmful when we finally got married, etc., how can we look differently at these seemingly outdated and guilt-provoking "teachings" and question them?

We need to visualize that fearful child who received so many wrong messages, and inform them firmly, but lovingly, that they are already a man/woman and that they are able to make the decisions that best fit their judgment as to the unique and independent individual they are.

This education has probably prevented us from living a fulfilling and happy life until now.

In short, can we adopt our own adult moral standards to guide our behaviors, rather than being held captive by "instructions" from the past if they are no longer relevant, cause us pain and promote guilt?

It is important to stress that there is a repeated theme in these few suggestions: the total and unconditional acceptance of ourselves.

As human beings, we don't start our journey with the intention of making mistakes, though, inevitably, we will. But unless our moral "transgressions" could be viewed as pure evil (in which case it is doubtful that we would be reading this book because psychopaths have showed to not be interested in improving), we are certainly worthy of our own compassion. And, with enough self-esteem and unconditional love, we will discover out that there are fewer things for which we need to ask forgive ourselves for forgiveness.

Angela, 35, is a decorator for a well-known supermarket chain. The eldest of five children, she belonged to a family strictly educated in the Catholic religion, with a strong emphasis on responsibility ... and guilt.

Her childhood memories always linked to the care of her younger brothers. They were all male, privileged in the treatment they received from their parents, imbued by a culture of socially accepted macho attitudes. This made her feel displaced in the world, her needs and desires postponed, but she never allowed herself to express it, even to her closest friends. She felt selfish even just thinking about it. The inner discomfort was growing, but the guilt covered it all, silencing everything.

When a new director arrived at work, she felt some patterns emerging: out of hours assignments became more frequent, as did sexist comments, and being treated differently from her male colleagues ...

Angela was the ideal employee: She was conscientious and hard working. However, she took responsibility for the mistakes of others. She almost invited them to take advantage of her situation, and there was there was always someone who actually did. Until one day, enough was enough. She asked for some time off. She sought help from me, started supervised antidepressant therapy and psychological treatment.

The road was long and arduous. She learned to say no to others (sometimes feeling a certain vindictive pleasure in it); she eventually returned to work and began to put a series of conditions into motion, all of them reasonable requests that could only be accepted by her director, because she was a very valued employee.

She then decided to make some changes in her family unit, too. This came to light after they had confronted her about how little she cared for them.

She calmly suggested that they should call any of her siblings if they needed something, because she was busy enjoying her new life. Then, to her parents' astonishment, she closed the door behind her. She stood on the threshold, feeling the familiar aftertaste of ingrained guilt urging her to go back in and ask for forgiveness.

Instead, she got in her car, started the engine, and left. With a big, satisfied smile on her face.

24. Understand that it's not possible to be happy all the time

Not everybody has to be happy all the time.
That's not mental health. That's crap.
—Dr. Meredith Grey,
***Grey'sanatomy*, Season 4**

Nowadays, it seems more unpopular than ever to be unhappy. People look at us in a funny way when we don't go around spilling over with joy and satisfaction. When they see us sad or thoughtful, they try to help us with common expressions such as "Come on! You have to be positive!" Certain self-help books will try to "fix us" even though we're probably not broken, and we can't be. Others will charge us a small fortune in workshops to teach us to smile more often.

The mission of advertisers is to make us need and desire *more* (usually material things). And the most common tactic they use is to convince us that buying their merchandise or service will make us more satisfied. Happiness according to them, is based on a variation of the principle of pleasure, which states that we seek to feel less pain and more pleasurable states. That is, we want to have many good experiences (if not excellent ones!)—taking shape through events and occurrences that put smiles on our faces. At the same time, we circumvent those experiences that could cause us sadness or anger.

Although a definition of happiness rooted in the principle of pleasure is accepted as a common standard, however, it is worth questioning it.

There is the idea that, ideally, we should live the life of Adam and Eve in Paradise, walking around with nothing to worry about (aside from staying away from those damned apples). But, should that be our natural state?

Human beings by nature fluctuate between different feelings. Emotion is always in motion—it's the result of unconscious processes that we never fully understand. Obsessively focusing on feeling happy is an act of self-denial and a refusal to accept the diversity of sensations available along with our history.

Moods are often affected by many external factors. To some extent (past certain limits, it becomes something pathological like in the case of bipolar disorder or cyclothymia), it is reasonable and human. What is not realistic is the expectation that we all have to roam around smiling like idiots, to uphold a set of false standards that are often imposed on us.

It is a paradox that the harder we seek happiness, the more it escapes us, but why should we aspire to be happy all the time? Maybe it isn't so much what we want for ourselves, but what we think others want from us. We might believe that if we're not always happy, then we will not be lovable and we will have no friends. Maybe it is the fear of loneliness or isolation that lies in all of us that drives us in the search for our happiness. We should never underestimate the powerful gregarious instincts that drives us to belong to groups and to seek recognition from our fellow men. The most relevant question here is: **what's wrong with feeling anger, fear, or sadness from time to time?** If we are not able to accept or respect the validity and necessity of these other feelings, then there is a part of our being that does not feel comfortable and, in principle, that is conflicting with happiness.

Sometimes (as long as it's not a pathological sadness, which indicates depression) being temporarily and reasonably sad can ultimately add substance and depth to our lives. But we are not generally encouraged to actually feel, as our emotions often serve to disturb other people and threaten to uncover the fear/sadness/anxiety they also experience and often try to avoid and cover up.

If we were to convince ourselves that anger and sadness are bad emotions and, therefore, we should not feel them, we would only deny ourselves a natural and healthy response. In fact, in the long run, suppressing our emotions will only prevent our happiness and peace of mind.

So, if we embrace sadness and anger as emotions worthy of expression, how do we know we are expressing them in the right way? Depending on the difficulties we face, our response will vary. Whether it's anger or sadness or frustration, healthy expressions of negative emotions have two components: firstly, they don't hurt us or others; and secondly, they can make us feel better about ourselves, not worse. A clear example is mourning the passing of a loved one: It hurts no one and it makes us feel better.

True happiness requires being in touch with our emotions and embracing, rather than rejecting or denying, what we have before us. In fact, by accepting what life presents to us, rather than labeling it as good or bad, we gain clarity. And this clarity allows us to refuse to make decisions based on wanting more of one thing and less of another.
That way, we realize that happiness is possible no matter what happens to us.

A 2017 article titled "The Secret of Happiness, Feeling Good or Feeling Right," [16] published in the *Journal of Experimental Psychology*, reports the findings of a study of 2,324 university undergraduates in 8 countries. The researchers discovered that people might be more satisfied when they feel the emotions they covet, regardless of whether those coveted emotions are pleasant or unpleasant. In other words, feeling our feelings is essential; it matters much more than whether they are positive or negative.

Our lack of both satisfaction with our present and hope for our future is what keeps us motivated, while the warm and fuzzy memories of the past reaffirm to us that the feelings we seek can still be found. In fact, living in constant happiness would completely shatter our will to achieve anything. When we find ourselves in the darkness, we seek for the light, and it is precisely this vital search what gives sense and purpose to our lives. **Nobody may be able to be happy all the time, but every time we scratch the surface to find a little bit of new happiness, we're paving the way to the next step of our lives. Because, deep down, what it's all about is making some sense of our own existence.**

25. Don't put all hope into medication

Pain could be killed. Sadness could not, but the drugs did shut its mouth for a time.
          —Colson Whitehead, *Zone One*

In the case of mild depressive disorders or reaction to life situations, the temptation to entrust our well-being to chemicals is significant (for both patients and professionals). Still, it can come at a high cost and not only in financial terms or concerning side effects; it sometimes encourages the idea that people are unable to find solutions on their own, by taking away our autonomy and leaving us more vulnerable to usual or banal vital circumstances that arise.

We live in an age of immediacy, in which, and by various factors, our levels of tolerancc to frustration in general are becoming lower.

Many people come to consultation with high expectations regarding as to what mental health professionals can do for them, at times **delegating responsibility for their well-being and resigning a more active role in their path to recovery.**

An increasing number of patients seek the existence of a holy grail in psychopharmaceuticals: Looking for "A pill that lifts my spirit, reduces my irritability, leaves me calmer, but does not leave me like a zombie and does not produce any secondary side effects ..."

The limit of pathological anxiety is often marked by subjectivity and is very influenced by culture. In some societies, any degree of stress is experienced as negative. In others, it is considered of little importance. The red line can be drawn when the person who suffers from the said anxiety is no longer able to function in their everyday life.

Some people, as we mentioned in the previous chapter, have too-high expectations with regard to their mood and worry if they're not happy all the time, whatever the circumstances. Some people find it difficult to understand, on the other hand, that a certain degree of anxiety is essential because it can be an adaptive feature and because, if we know how to listen, it tells us interesting things about ourselves and about the world in which we live. In addition, anxiety is a mechanism of social cohesion; it is a generator of solidarity.

It is of great importance to think twice before seeking medication from your doctor because oftentimes the symptom is treated, but the cause of the problem remains buried.

At other times, antidepressant and anxiolytic drugs are necessary, but there is little point in expecting them to do all the work on their own. We have to complement the treatment by developing a more proactive attitude and by practicing acceptance, or by undergoing a short period of psychotherapy.

Every patient who suffers from a mood/anxiety disorder should leave the clinic with a "proactive list" not only including physical exercise or changes to their eating or sleep habits, but it should also include pleasurable activities or postponed tasks. The list should be approached with a fighting spirit, understanding that, just like any other kind of training or preparation, these modifications will bring a wealth of benefits in time.

Gemma is an intelligent 21-year-old pharmacy student. She lives with her parents and has what can be described as a somewhat insecure personality.

She was referred to me by her primary care physician with a diagnosis of "agoraphobia" (aversion to open spaces) as, lately, she'd had a difficult time socializing with her friends and preferred to stay at home more than usual.

During the interview, Gemma confessed that being faced with her diagnosis was very frightening and she had been advised by her GP that an antidepressant could deal with the problem.

After discussions, we agreed that her situation was directly linked with the anxiety caused by an upcoming examination along with a recent relationship breakup which she had not attributed to her levels of stress.

We worked with Gemma on the importance of understanding that she contained the emotional tools needed to deal with the healing process and that there was no sign that she couldn't make it through and overcome her insecurities.

At the end of the consultation she acknowledged, with tears in her eyes, that what had scared her the most was the possibility that there was "something wrong" with her personality that she could not solve. She had also felt panicked by the potential side effects of the drugs prescribed.

The prospect of starting a psychopharmacological treatment was seen by Gemma as both her relief ... and her condemnation.

Eventually, the situation improved on its own, but a lot of the work was done before she left the clinic: Gemma went home with the idea that she herself had the means to deal with her own problems.

Conclusion

If you have managed to read all the chapters of this book, you will have discovered that three basic components often arise in the different methods proposed: good **self-observation** (with many notes to take and things to write), **progressive staged change planning, and insistence on deprogramming unproductive behaviors learned over the years**, without wasting time by seeking causes. These are **three critical levers** for long-term change in most emotional or behavioral disorders. They require some discipline, but we can expect excellent results if we persist with our efforts to change, improve and heal.

I would also like to emphasize three additional points that I find essential in the process of change and self-therapy.

The first is *general **attitude*** that we must try to adopt toward ourselves; we must become as benevolent and as tolerant as possible. Any form of guilt, shame, or denigration in the face of the difficulties we encounter is unnecessary and counterproductive. On the one hand, we should not have to feel guilty about the symptoms we suffer (although we do have to acknowledge responsibility for changing them) since their causes are usually multifactorial and often quite obscure. On the other hand, there is no human being who lacks vulnerability (let's remember that the prevalence of mental disorders in the population is around 25% to 30% and continues to grow). Therefore, it is necessary to show great self-compassion so as not to add more suffering to our struggles, and to be better able to fight these problems over time.

The second point, which complements the first one, is the importance of ***determination to change***. Recognizing vulnerabilities does not mean remaining helpless or surrendering to them. It is possible and vital to fight in order to improve our quality of life and, in some cases, to get rid of unnecessary pain. But this struggle, depending on the problem itself and how long it's been there, can be long and arduous, with ups and downs and, therefore, possible moments of discouragement. It is here that strength of determination is essential: never question the purpose of change, never give up, and always continue to pursue our goals. Of course, it's understandable that we have to take some "time out" in this game, but this shouldn't lead us to give up and we should resume our journey as soon as possible. Remember that it is necessary to rely on small improvements, as if these steps were part of a long staircase that serve to strengthen our motivation and keep hope alive.

The last point is **_humor_**, which can be made a resource as much as necessary, at any time and in any circumstance. People who are able to dedramatize, enjoy the absurdity of the world and everyday life, are those who prove to be the most resistant to adversity and stress. Feeling joy, being able to laugh at ourselves and our problems, and adopting a frank but straightforward attitude are the best defenses against anxiety, boredom, and dark ideas. Humor is beneficial for the body and mind (probably due to the release of neurotransmitters with antagonistic effects towards the substances released by stress). Humor allows us to connect as humans to each other through irreplaceable positive emotions. Learning the habit of viewing the comical side of any situation is the best means for pushing back any inner demons, which inevitably tend to occupy places in our minds ... if we leave them!

Let's adopt a sense of humor towards our mishaps, our phobias, even our manias, anger, and irritability. It is the first step to defeating them!

References

1. Emmons Robert A., McCullough Michael E. (2004), The Psychology of Gratitude, Oxford University Press, USA.

2. Brickman, Philip & Coates, Dan & Janoff-Bulman, Ronnie. (1978). Lottery Winners and Accident Victims: Is Happiness Relative? Journal of personality and social psychology. 36. 917-27. 10.1037/0022-3514.36.8.917.

3. Jebb, Andrew & Tay, Louis & Diener, Ed & Oishi, Shigehiro. (2018). Happiness, Income Satiation, and Turning Points Around the World. Nature Human Behavior. 2. 33–38. 10.1038/s41562-017-0277-0.

4. Torre Pablo S. (March 23, 2009). "How (and Why) Athletes Go Broke". Sports Illustrated. Archived from the originalon 2009-08-11.

5. Mullainathan, Sendhil and Eldar. Shafir. (2013) Scarcity: Why Having Too Little Means so Much. New York: Times Books, Henry Holt and Company.

6. Hill, Andrew & Curran, Thomas. (2015). Multidimensional Perfectionism and Burnout: A Meta-Analysis. Personality and Social Psychology Review. 20. 10.1177/1088868315596286.

7. Dorland, W. A. N. (2007). Dorland's illustrated medical dictionary. Philadelphia, PA: Saunders.

8. Wilding Christine , Milne Aileen. (2008) Cognitive Behavioural TherapyTeach Yourself Books.

9. Cornaglia J, "Acectar". (2008). Editions des Vosges.

10. Ware, Bronnie. The Top Five Regrets of the Dying: A Life Transformed by the Dearly Departing (2012), Carlsbad, CA: Hay House, Inc.

11. Goldstein Pavel, Weissman-Foge Irit , Guillaume , Dumas Simone G.Shamay-Tsoory. Brain-to-brain coupling during handholding is associated with pain reduction. Proceedings of the National Academy of Sciences Mar 2018, 115 (11) E2528-2537; DOI:10.1073/pnas.1703643115

12. Frankl Viktor, (1999), El hombre en busca del sentido último: el análisis existencial y la conciencia espiritual del ser humano,Paidós Ibérica,

13. Maddi, S.R. (1987) Hardiness Training at Illinois Bell Telephone. In: Opatz, J.P., Ed., Health Promotion Evaluation, National Wellness Institute, Stevens Point, 101-115.

14. Camille B Wortman, Roxane Cohen Silver,The myths of coping with loss Journal of Consulting and Clinical Psychology1989/6/30

15. Ellis Albert, (1961), A Guide to Rational Living. Englewood Cliffs, N.J., Prentice-Hall.

16. Tamir Maya,Schwartz Shalom.The Secret to Happiness: Feeling Good or Feeling Right? Journal of Experimental Psychology General, 146(10), 1448-1459, October 2017